"This book was a much-needed gift to my weary and news-battered heart. In a time when we are constantly being told that we are more divided and combative than ever and that the future will bring only more calamity and despair, Chris Anderson presents an inspiring body of evidence to support the tremendous and transformative power of generosity—that most beautiful of human impulses. *Infectious Generosity* is a combination of inarguable data and incredibly moving stories. How wonderful to learn that seemingly small and humble acts of kindness can create exponential whirlwinds of benevolent impact, and that generosity is just as contagious as any virus! I flew through these pages with an increasing sense of joy, and was left inspired and hopeful."
—**ELIZABETH GILBERT,** AUTHOR OF *EAT, PRAY, LOVE*

"Profound and compelling, this book is a masterpiece, and an important one. I want everyone I know to read this and act on it in some way, too."

AUTHOR ... OLOGY

"Truly inspiring ... This book is the first page-turner ever written about human generosity. It will change the way you see the world around you."
—**ELIZABETH DUNN,** SOCIAL PSYCHOLOGIST AND EXPERT ON THE SCIENCE OF HAPPINESS

"Concise and profound, this truly excellent book is going to have a big impact on the key issues of our times."
—**ALAIN DE BOTTON,** AUTHOR AND PHILOSOPHER

"A beautiful book—lucid, warm, intelligent, and persuasive."
—**STEVEN PINKER,** AUTHOR AND PROFESSOR OF PSYCHOLOGY, HARVARD UNIVERSITY

"Warning: Reading this book may give you an irresistible urge to get up and take action. This is simply a wonderful book."
—**RUTGER BREGMAN,** AUTHOR OF *HUMANKIND*

BY CHRIS ANDERSON

Infectious Generosity

TED Talks

INFECTIOUS
GENEROSITY

INFECTIOUS
GENEROSITY

The Ultimate Idea Worth Spreading

CHRIS ANDERSON

CROWN
NEW YORK

Published in the United States by Crown, an imprint of the Crown Publishing Group, a division of Penguin Random House LLC, New York.

CROWN and the Crown colophon are registered trademarks of Penguin Random House LLC.

Illustrations by Liana Finck

LIBRARY OF CONGRESS CATALOGING-IN-PUBLICATION DATA
Names: Anderson, Chris, author.
Title: Infectious generosity / Chris Anderson.
Description: New York: Crown, [2024] | Includes bibliographical references.
Identifiers: LCCN 2023034130 (print) | LCCN 2023034131 (ebook) |
ISBN 9780593727553 (hardcover) | ISBN 9780593735138 |
ISBN 9780593727560 (ebook)
Subjects: LCSH: Generosity.
Classification: LCC BJ1533.G4 A594 2024 (print) | LCC BJ1533.G4 (ebook) |
DDC 177/.7—dc23/eng/20231003
LC record available at https://lccn.loc.gov/2023034130
LC ebook record available at https://lccn.loc.gov/2023034131

Hardback ISBN 978-0-593-72755-3
International edition ISBN 978-0-593-73513-8
Ebook ISBN 978-0-593-72756-0

Printed in the United States of America on acid-free paper

crownpublishing.com

2 4 6 8 9 7 5 3 1

First Edition

Book design by Jo Anne Metsch

To those who give, and to those who will . . .

CONTENTS

INTRODUCTION

You wouldn't think that a cluster of atoms weighing less than one-trillionth of a gram could amount to much. Yet one such cluster, following a tiny tweak to its shape, entered a human body in late 2019, sparking a chain of events that killed more than seven million people and shut down the world economy.

Among the many lessons of Covid-19, one of the most profound is this: You don't need to be big to be powerful. You just need to be *infectious*.

Any pattern that can replicate itself can have unlimited impact. Coronaviruses do it by avoiding human immune systems, creating billions of copies of themselves, and then triggering us to cough or sneeze those copies into other people's air supply.

But many other types of infection are possible.

I want to persuade you that one such possible contagion could actually transform the world for the better. Its name? *Generosity*. If we figured out how to make generosity truly infectious, it could turn the tide on the growing divisiveness of our world and usher in a new era of hope.

Generosity? Really?!

It's an odd word, to be sure. A little old-fashioned, perhaps. It seems, on first blush, too soft a force to be deployed against the challenges we're facing. You, as an individual, may be as generous as you like, but how can your well-intentioned individual gestures and sacrifices amount to anything?

But that's the whole point. They can. Any generous act can have extraordinary impact *if* it can make the leap from isolated to infectious. With a few little tweaks to their shape, acts of generosity can become explosively powerful. This book is devoted to showing you how.

Generosity's infectious potential draws from two key drivers: human nature and the connectedness of the modern era. In the chapters that follow, I'll describe how overlooked traits that lie deep inside every human can combine to create chain reactions of generous behavior. And how these ripple effects can be turbocharged by the Internet for world-changing impact.

The Internet is of course famous for enabling contagions of all kinds, from social media memes to viral marketing. As with a virus, humans are the vector for the Internet's infectiousness. Instead of replicating in noses and lungs, words and images ignite in our brains, provoking our fingers to press Like or Share.

Alas, many of the contagions that spread online are not healthy. Fueled by ad-driven business models that seek to glue people to their screens, social media platforms have turned the web into an outrage-generating machine. Instead of seeing the best in one another, we're often seeing the worst, and it's driving us apart.

I'll be tackling this problem head-on. Along with many others, I used to dream of the Internet as a force for bringing people together. And I'm not willing to let that dream go. I believe there's a pathway to reclaiming a healthier Internet, with infectious generosity playing a starring role.

In fact, this book is anchored by two complementary themes: *The Internet can turbocharge generosity* and *Generosity can transform the Internet.* Each theme feeds the other. If we see the Internet as a scary, inhuman mass of strangers ready to judge and exploit us, it will be hard for us to trust it with our good intentions. But without people making efforts to connect with others online in a generous spirit, the Internet can't deliver its potential as a force for good. It's tempting to dismiss the Internet today as a downward spiral of toxicity. What is desperately needed is for us to start an upward cycle in which the growing visibility of a more generous version of humanity inspires people to play their part in contributing to the common good.

I feel a real sense of urgency about this. We're in the early stages of seeing our world turned upside down by artificial intelligence. Guess what the source of the power of AI is? It's the Internet. In essence, the most powerful AI systems are designed to digest the sum of what humans have posted online and create predictive models. Do we want to rely on AI trained with today's Internet? No! We really don't. We'll risk amplifying much that is dangerous. If we can find a way to nudge the Internet to a kinder, more generous, more positive place, it could have an incalculable impact on our future, both directly and by providing a healthier foundation for AI.

It may seem absurd to you to imagine us humans, with all our imperfections, ever overcoming the Internet's woes: division, disinformation, data surveillance, addiction, social media–fueled insecurity, and so much more. I hear you. But I invite you to suspend judgment just for a bit. Under the radar, there are remarkable things afoot. They're worth learning about.

Moreover, we *must* take on this problem. I see no choice. Our whole collective future is at stake. Paradoxically, the very urgency of the problem may help us. The greater the sense of crisis, the more humans shift from *me* to *we*. We're in a moment when people are *really* worried. I think that means we're also craving things that could draw us together.

The good news is that the ingredients to infectious generosity are hiding in plain sight. Simple, ordinary, unremarkable human kindness, for example, now has the potential to ripple outward like never before.

Take the following story. You're sitting in your car at an intersection when a rainstorm hits. You notice two people by the side of the road getting soaked. One of them is in a wheelchair. So you jump out of the car, run to them, and give them your umbrella. No doubt, acts like this have happened countless times throughout history between people stuck outside in rainstorms. It might seem mundane.

However, when this act of kindness happened in Washington, DC, in 2022, a stranger in another car captured it on video. When the clip was posted online, it attracted millions of views and more than ninety thousand likes on Reddit. Comments from inspired viewers poured out: *"I wanna be like him." "Gives me hope." "If he did that to me I'd feel the inescapable urge to pay it forward." "I'm going to start carrying extra umbrellas."*

An act that, pre-Internet, might have meant something to just three people ended up inspiring a multitude.

But an instance of everyday kindness captured on a viral video is just one example of infectious generosity. There are countless other ways to ignite it. Everyone can do something that has the *potential* to spread: A retired engineer posting invaluable know-how on You-Tube. An artist sharing work that provokes and enchants. An act of human courage that inspires millions of people on social media. A company that offers free courses on a technical subject in which it has expertise. A storyteller who highlights a powerful cause that an online community can fund. Or just someone who wakes up grateful for something in their life and decides to pay it forward, sparking an online chain reaction.

TRENDSETTER

As head of TED for the past twenty years, I've had a ringside view of many of the world's most significant discoveries, inventions, technologies, and ideas. A friend asked why I chose this specific topic to write a book about. My answer was that I've come to see generosity as *the* essential connecting thread between the most important lessons I've ever learned—as an individual, as the leader of an organization, and as a citizen of the world. For years, TED's tagline has been "ideas worth spreading," and I have come to believe that generosity is the ultimate idea worth spreading.

How can that be? Does it even make sense to call generosity an idea? Wouldn't it be more apt to call it a virtue or a character trait? Well, it's certainly those things. But it's also a giant, glittering idea, and arguably the best idea humans have ever embraced. *It is the idea that we should make efforts on behalf of others, not just ourselves.*

As we'll see, generosity is fueled by deep biological instincts. But those instincts are fragile. They need to be strengthened and shaped by our reflective minds. In every religion and in almost every culture there has been an effort to elevate the role of generosity, because it is the key to realizing our potential. It is generosity that inspires reciprocal trust and makes cooperation possible. Cooperation is what allowed us to create civilization. Generosity is therefore core to all that humanity has built, and to what we might yet build in the future.

Of course, building thriving societies took more than generosity alone. We needed many other drivers, including the rule of law and regulated markets. These have played a key role in constraining nongenerous aspects of human nature and turning them into something productive for the common good. Adam Smith's wonder at the benevolent effects of people trading with one another is well taken. It really is incredible that millions of people working largely in their own self-interest can create benefits for everyone.

But history reveals that every institution we've ever built has been subject to flaws and needs constant tweaking and improvement. Usually those improvements have been driven by people who are passionate about the common good, reformers and advocates fueled by a generous public spirit. This is how we've fought back against child labor, slavery, price gouging, pollution, and unfair exploitation of all kinds—fights that continue to this day. The Internet has the potential to be as significant an invention for humanity as regulated markets or the rule of law. It connects us all and opens the door to unlimited human potential. But in its current state, it is deeply flawed. The Internet is crying out for generous-minded reformers who can reclaim it as an amplifier of kindness instead of meanness. Because of the power of infectiousness, each of us can contribute more than we know.

Indeed, perhaps the simplest, most powerful moral question people can ask of their own lives is this: *Am I a net giver or a net taker?* The answer to that question will come from taking stock of our lives. The people we've hurt versus the people we've helped. The resources we've consumed versus those we've protected. The ugliness we've been part of versus the beauty we've created. And so on. It's an intensely personal question—and it has consequences for all of us. Whether our collective future is a good one or not depends largely on whether the majority of people give more to the world than they take from it.

Generosity has played a key role in building the tools, the ideas, and the institutions that have allowed civilization to flourish. But it is also essential for something else: our personal happiness. Generosity is a key ingredient for a contented life. People often tell me the main reason they watch TED Talks is to answer this question: How can I be my best self? They say that speakers inspire them to think more expansively about how they may contribute to the world.

All of this is why I've come to see generosity as central to everything that matters. And because we're living in an age when one person's generosity has the potential to infect others without limit, there's a whole new reason to spread this idea far and wide.

Doing so isn't always easy, however. Right now, our collective future seems dangerously fragile, given the ugliness of much of modern culture. There's a real possibility that we will withdraw from one another and abandon the greatest idea we've ever had. But there's also a scenario in which we rediscover it, and amplify it like never before.

There are so many different ways to be generous. It's not just about giving away money. Simply adopting a generous mindset can make a difference. That can lead to gifts of time, talent, creativity, connection, and basic human kindness. These gifts have always been part of what it is to be a good human. But today they have the potential to create amazing chain reactions.

Money matters, too, of course. In the pages ahead, we'll discover how to go beyond instinctive acts of charity to thoughtful giving that dramatically amplifies the impact of what you spend, via the Internet and in other ways.

And if all this still seems daunting or impossible, remember that you don't have to do it alone. Many of the most powerful and beautiful examples of generosity happen when people join forces: a giving circle, a local volunteer group, or an online collective.

Whoever you are, the potential for generosity—as we'll discover—is wired deep inside you. Indeed, it's possible that your quest to become a net giver will surprise you with a renewed sense of meaning, purpose, and joyful hope. *It's who I'm meant to be.*

This is also true for organizations, whether for-profit or nonprofit. One of the surprises of the Internet age is that generous acts often turn out to be the smartest, most satisfying decisions an organization can make.

We're taught to think of generosity as an act done purely for selfless reasons. But I'll make the case that it can be much more than that. Today, more than ever, the decision to be generous can be simultaneously an act of sacrifice and, profoundly, an act in the long-term self-interest of the giver. The people who are generous are the people who will come to enjoy the deepest happiness. And the companies and organizations that are generous are the companies and organizations that will own the future.

If we could pay a little more attention to generosity's potential for contagion and grow a little more creative and courageous in how we contribute to that potential, we could be transformed—in our personal lives and in our families, our neighborhoods, our businesses, and our nonprofit organizations.

We'd open the door to thrilling new human possibility.

*   *   *

The book has three parts: "Why," "How," and "What If?"

Part 1 is devoted to understanding *why* infectious generosity's time has come. I share the remarkable sequence of events at TED that convinced me that the Internet has changed the rules of generosity far more than I had realized, and the three big principles that I learned from those events. Then we dive into new learnings about human nature and how the call of generosity can bring us both surprising consequences and profound happiness. I give the inside story of the "Mystery Experiment," the biggest social science study yet that demonstrates how kindness begets kindness.

In part 2 we explore *how* to turn this theory into action. We look at what it takes to create a generous mindset, the many types of giving that can turn into something much bigger, and how we can share stories of generosity with one another. There's an important chapter on financial giving, including how to tap into different forms of leverage to significantly amplify the impact of our money.

Then in part 3 we ask *what if* our world had generosity more deeply embedded in it. We'll plot how to take back the Internet so that it can realize the dream millions of us once had, to help humankind be both human and kind. We'll look at how companies and organizations may be transformed by generosity. We'll ponder how to empower our greatest changemakers to embark on truly audacious plans for change. We'll explore the case for a pledge that everyone in the world could take that would carry us all on a shared journey of generosity. And finally we'll ponder how we might embed a generosity mindset inside our future selves.

One thing I deliberately *won't* address is public policy. It's clearly true that for many of the world's worst problems, governments have a key role to play. I have huge admiration for those both inside and outside government who are focused on those issues. Those debates dominate most of our public conversation spaces. And they matter. But they aren't my focus here. This book is about what *we* can do.

Whoever you are and wherever you are, I hope you will come on this journey with me. There's a good chance you'll become infected by something powerful, something that could impact how you spend some of your future time, money, and creativity. And this something just may end up infecting others.

But this is a healthy infection. A beautiful, hopeful, healthy infection. You may wish never to recover.

PART ONE

WHY

Why Infectious Generosity's time has come . . .

INSIDE A CONTAGION

The surprising aftermath of a decision to give

Let me share with you the experience that opened my eyes to the Internet's potential to turbocharge generosity.

I'm a media entrepreneur. For the first half of my career, I built a company in the UK and the US that published scores of hobbyist magazines, many of them about technology. In 1998 I was invited to attend a conference in California that, unusually, was devoted not to one industry but to three: technology, entertainment, and design. Yup, this was the TED conference.

Because of the conference's breadth of content, speakers had to make their work accessible to outsiders, and it turns out that when you do that, there is a crossover effect. Software creators were inspired by physical architecture, screenwriters and artists had their minds blown by technologists, and everyone felt the potential and significance of their work to be elevated. I was mesmerized.

A couple of years later, I had the opportunity to take over the conference from its charismatic co-founder. I leaped at the chance—partly because there seemed to be good prospects of expanding its sphere. It wasn't just technology, entertainment, and design that could cross-pollinate with one another; it was every subject. All human knowledge is part of a single elusive reality. We don't fully understand anything until we understand how it connects to the other parts of knowledge.

I couldn't afford to buy TED personally—the dot-com bust of 2000–2001 had ravaged my media company, Future plc. So, instead, TED became part of a not-for-profit foundation I had created a few years earlier, when times were good. And I left Future to focus full-time on this weird conference and to ponder how it might grow.

Since it was now a nonprofit, TED had to be run for the public good. And that meant trying to find a way to gain a wider audience for the inspirational talks that were given there. In the early aughts, this was harder than you may think.

We tried to persuade TV networks that TED Talks would make for excellent viewing. They laughed at us. Public lectures were about the most boring thing they could imagine. Then we had a more radical idea.

The Experiment

On the Internet, bandwidth was relentlessly increasing, and the fledgling technology of online video was starting to become viable. Back in 2006, it was often limited to a small low-res window in the corner of a desktop screen, but we felt it was worth a try. In an experiment, we posted six of the talks in full on our website.

To our surprise, they went viral, rapidly notching up tens of thousands of views. Not much by today's standards, but for a website that had been getting just a few hundred visitors a day, it was startling. And the feedback we received from viewers shocked us in its intensity. People didn't just like what they had seen. They loved it. They'd been inspired. And suddenly we were faced with a dilemma. As a nonprofit, we felt we had an obligation to freely share *all* of our best content online.

Now, this was clearly a dangerous move. Our attendees paid a lot of money to come to TED. That was by far the main source of income we had. Why would they continue to do that if the content was freely available on the Internet?

We weren't sure. But we went ahead anyway.

The Response

What happened next was astonishing.

First, the bulk of our conference-going community quickly got behind the move. A small handful grumbled, but the vast majority were thrilled that they could now share a profound experience with others.

And the response from those viewing these talks for the first time online was even more surprising. We were deluged with messages from people expressing how deeply they'd been moved, and how they wanted to help support the speakers and further help spread their ideas.

Visits to our website exploded into the millions, and TED was transformed from a niche conference to a global brand—all via word of mouth. Instead of demand for our conference being destroyed, it increased.

And something else happened: From all over the world we started receiving offers to translate the talks into local languages. Once we'd set up a system to facilitate this, literally thousands of volunteer translators got to work, collaborating in pairs so that they could verify each other's work. Seventeen years later, TED Talks have been translated into more than one hundred languages by some fifty thousand generous souls.

What the Internet Taught Us

This was a lot to take in. We had made the decision to give away our talks mostly out of a sense of obligation—our nonprofit's mission was to share valuable knowledge freely with the world. But what we got back was transformative. The Internet had spread TED Talks far and wide, generating millions, and then billions, of online views, attracting significant sponsorship revenue. Over the next three years, TED's income multiplied more than tenfold, allowing us to ponder exciting new possibilities.

To shape those possibilities, a guiding principle came into focus. Back then, we called it radical openness. But today I think of it simply as, yes, *infectious generosity*. The Internet had taught us that if you gave away the biggest thing you could think of, you would be amazed at what came back.

So we asked ourselves: Beyond our content, what else could we give away?

First we founded a fellows program to bring to TED a global group of extraordinary thinkers and doers who couldn't otherwise afford to come. This program rapidly became worth its weight in gold when an early fellow, Logan Smalley, an educator, approached us with the idea of launching a series of short animated videos to share knowledge and spark curiosity in learners of all ages. His TED-Ed program was itself powered by generosity. Teachers and animators gave their services for free or at reduced costs, and visionary donors covered the rest of the cost. Since 2011, Logan's team has ended up creating more than fifteen hundred animations, many of which have won awards and are now used in tens of thousands of schools, and millions of homes, creating more than a billion sparks of curiosity every year.

The TEDx Surprise

But undoubtedly the biggest risk we took was to give away our *brand*. The TED name itself. Lots of people had been inquiring about the possibility of having a TED conference in their own city. We couldn't imagine how to do this. So we decided to let them do it themselves. We issued free licenses to organizers around the world. They could call it a TED event and thereby make it far easier to recruit both speakers and audiences. We just added a little asterisk to the brand in the form of an *x*. TEDx was intended to mean *TED self-organized in location x,* but the deeper meaning of the *x* turned out to be TED multiplied or even TED turned exponential.

Instead of TED being just a single annual event, there were suddenly hundreds, and then thousands, of events. Each event was put on by a local team who volunteered prodigious amounts of time and talent. They brought TED to movie theaters, universities, sports stadiums, opera houses, parliaments—as well as places we could never have imagined: rainforests, prisons, refugee camps. We had given away our brand, but to us, the generosity of the response seemed far more astonishing.

To many business advisers at the time, all this seemed crazy. *Harvard Business Review* even published an article on it, provocatively titled "When TED Lost Control of Its Crowd." But the "loss" was deliberate. Yes, there were occasions when events bombed or an inadequately prepared speaker created embarrassment. But these were surprisingly rare. And over time the whole system improved. Local organizers gained invaluable experience and shared what they were learning with us and with one another.

TEDx brought remarkable voices to the world that we would probably never have discovered ourselves. Some of the most popular TED speakers of all time—including Brené Brown and Simon Sinek—were discovered at TEDx events.

And as I write, some fifteen years later, the decision to give away our brand seems like the wisest thing we could ever have done. More than twenty-five thousand TEDx events have been held. They've created an online archive of more than two hundred thousand talks. And those talks attract more than a billion views annually. A central team of just twelve people oversees the whole operation, offering guidance and training, and upholding adherence to our mission.

Using a traditional command-and-control structure, you could never build an events organization of anything like this scale with just twelve people. This is an operation made possible only because of the magic of infectious generosity. We gave away our brand and our advice. And what we got back was a worldwide knowledge-spreading miracle.

An Endless Ripple

We are still, to this day, learning of new ripple effects from the decisions to give away our content and our brand. Take one of those first six talks that we released. It was by an educator, Sir Ken Robinson, arguing that schools needed to do more to nurture creativity and curiosity in children. The talk is hilarious—and deeply inspiring. He delivered it to a theater of five hundred people. But as I write, some seventeen years after its release, more than five thousand people are viewing it every single day. And the stories told by some of those people take my breath away. For example, members of the performance-art troupe Blue Man Group decided to invest in a new private school in New York City that would implement Sir Ken's ideas. Countless others were inspired to become teachers, and teachers were motivated to change how they taught.

In 2022 I met a woman who may have created the biggest ripple effect of all. Her name is Supriya Paul. Ten years earlier she was a university student in India, preparing to be an accountant, when her friend Shobhit Banga made her watch Sir Ken's talk. Supriya told me: "It was that moment that seeded the idea in our heads that we wanted to do something to solve India's education challenges—and not solve it for one or many individuals but for an entire generation." Because the two friends had been so inspired by a short video, they were determined to use this technique to realize these dreams. Supriya's father reluctantly agreed that she could delay being an accountant for a year to give it a shot.

Just in time, Supriya and Shobhit secured the funding needed for their new organization, Josh Talks. In Hindi *josh* means "vigor" or "strength of mind." And that is exactly what these talks are delivering. They're focusing on lower-income viewers who may otherwise lack access to good education. By sharing stories of relatable role models, Josh Talks is raising aspirations and unlocking the potential of people across the subcontinent. As of 2023, more than fifty million people in India watch Josh Talks every month in ten regional languages. And, in Supriya's words, "we're just getting started."

Josh Talks in turn is creating its own powerful ripple effects. Supriya told me about one of their viewers, twenty-year-old Manish. Right before the pandemic, Manish lost his house due to heavy floods in his village in Bihar. After Covid-19 hit India, his financial situation worsened, and he desperately looked for a way to support his family. During this time, Manish came across a Josh Talks video of Vivek Kumar, who, just like him, came from a small town and used his knowledge and skills to teach other children. The talk ignited a belief in him: "If he can do it, then so can I!" Manish started teaching children in his district. Now, just a couple of years later, he runs his own coaching institute and has helped scores of children successfully pass their tenth-grade exams, thereby paving the way for yet another wave of ripple effects. One twelfth-grader named Aman told Supriya, "Manish is a brilliant teacher. His passion and dedication inspire me every day to become the best version of myself."

In his talk, Sir Ken concluded by sharing his dream of the hopeful future that human imagination could usher in. "The only way we'll do it is by seeing our creative capacities for the richness they are and seeing our children for the hope that they are. And our task is to educate their whole being, so they can face this future. By the way, we may not see this future, but they will. And our job is to help them make something of it."

Indeed, Sir Ken passed away in 2021 and never learned about Supriya or Manish or Aman. But the ripple effects from his words will continue forever.

I know what you might be thinking. *Isn't TED an outlier? Surely, this outcome is unique to TED and its speakers.* We certainly had a lot going in our favor. We were able to attract a wonderful, talented team, willing to take risks. Extraordinary speakers like Sir Ken gave us their time and wisdom without seeking payment. And our timing was fortunate, offering this free content right when online video was taking off.

But TED is far from the only place where I've seen the multiplier effect of generosity take hold. I am convinced that the learnings from this experience apply broadly, both to organizations and to individuals. As we're about to see, the connected era changes the rules of generosity for everyone.

THE INFINITE VILLAGE

*Why global connection requires us
to rethink generosity*

As systems get bigger, there is often a dramatic step-change in how they behave. The first hundred, two hundred, or thousand drivers in a town will feel the freedom of the open road. But if that number suddenly grows to one hundred thousand, there's a new name for their experience: gridlock.

Extra scale can destroy quality, but it can also enhance it. A mid-size restaurant with only three customers is dead. Even those three won't come back. With thirty customers, it comes alive. All thirty are inadvertently signaling to one another that this is a place worth coming to. Uber is useless when there are not enough drivers in the network. But with hundreds in every city, it becomes remarkable.

Likewise, as the scale of human connection has increased, I believe we've hit a step-change in how we should think about generosity. We no longer live in the small groups that shaped our basic moral

instincts. Today we can connect to pretty much anyone. Our village spans the entire globe. And that changes everything.

There are three specific features of our connected era we take for granted, but when you look at them with fresh eyes and put them together, they create a whole new highly compelling logic for what we should hold on to and what may be given away.

1. What We Value Is Increasingly Nonmaterial

For most of history, gifts usually involved the transfer of atoms and molecules from one human to another. Food. Flowers. Tools. Clothes. Collectible objects.

But the past decades have seen a giant shift. More and more value in the world today comes not from the tangible but the intangible. Not atoms but bits. Not physical stuff but the unique creations of human minds. Physical things still underpin everything. But what matters increasingly is how they are shaped, patterned, organized.

Steel can be turned into an intricate machine. Paint can be turned into art. Electricity can be turned into computer programs. That patterning is where value is created. And patterns, per se, are nonmaterial. They're a form of information, of knowledge.

We were stunned that people were so excited to receive free TED Talks online. But we shouldn't have been. Information brings empowerment. Knowledge offers tools to improve our lives. An inspiring human in digital format can still inspire. Aesthetic creativity fills our souls with delight. Software and artificial intelligence have almost unlimited power to shape the future world.

Think of how you spend your day and what proportion of your time is absorbed by nonmaterial things. Reading your messages. Watching the news. Listening to podcasts. Zooming with colleagues or loved ones. Snapping photos. Turning to a search engine to unlock knowledge. Playing with an app. Streaming entertainment. Engaging with an AI.

If how we spend our time is a key measure of what we value, then what we value is—increasingly—intangible.

Of course, physical things still make up the fundamentals of life. You can't eat bits, drink software, or wear a video. We're on a planet where, to our collective shame, at least one billion of our fellow humans still lack food and shelter. Yet even in the battle to end global poverty, some of the most transformative changes of the past decades have been enabled by growing access to connectivity and to knowledge. And as people slowly obtain the means to meet their physical needs, a growing proportion of their time and attention turns to the nonmaterial.

2. Nonmaterial Things Can Be Given Away at Limitless Scale

Before online video, if you wanted to share an inspirational lecture with a large number of people, your best bet was to burn copies onto a bunch of DVDs and mail them out. That would cost two dollars or more per recipient. Today, the incremental cost of giving someone that same lecture is perhaps *one ten thousandth* of that. It's a tiny sliver of bandwidth. Essentially, it's free. And instantaneous.

And the same applies to all digital goods. Books, films, music, software, recipes, designs, educational courses, blueprints, profoundly original ideas, heartwarming stories—every type of intellectual property or knowledge. All can be offered to the world with effectively zero distribution costs.

If you can shape a gift into a digital form, the Internet makes it ridiculously easy to give it away to an unlimited number of recipients.

This news is decades old, but it still blows my mind. Once upon a time someone who spent several months creating something special could share it with only a few people. Now we can pass that same creation to people across the world. This means our collective potential for generosity has been increased by not just 10 percent or 50 percent but by orders of magnitude. It's not merely an improvement; it's a transformation.

And the exploding power of AI may be able to amplify that capability even further. Instead of one piece of content being shared with a million people, it will soon be possible to let AI personalize that content uniquely to each recipient.

These technologies help level the playing field. Traditionally, the most impactful acts of generosity were carried out by those with significant resources. If you wanted to reach a thousand people instead of one, you had to spend a thousand times as much. And few could do that. But in the online world, what makes something go viral and spread to millions is much more mysterious. It can be as much about imagination and ingenuity as about resources.

But wait, you may be thinking. *If it's so easy to give, is it really generosity?* Today's celebrities shouldn't boast about giving away a million candid pictures to their fans. Thirty years ago that would have been astonishing. Today it's just Instagram. Indeed, there's a whole world of influencers churning out their free content, all of it sponsored in some way.

Far from being recipients of generosity, aren't we all just drowning in content? Content that we're paying for with our attention and with our data, which cleverly drive all those ads?

It's true that today's cornucopia of free online content and services makes it easy to be blasé about the Internet's largesse; and if you spend all day in a forest, you forget how beautiful some individual trees truly are. But that's a shame, actually.

I think we can distinguish between online sharing that is purely transactional or promotional and that which has taken great effort to create and is offered in a genuine spirit of generosity. There are countless examples of the latter:

- Wildlife sound recordist Martyn Stewart has recorded nearly one hundred thousand pieces, consisting of thirty thousand hours of material, spread across forty countries. These include the call of an owl in a boreal forest, thunderstorms in the Australian outback, the soundscape of a Costa Rican rainforest, and the croak of the Panamanian golden frog. After being diagnosed with cancer, he made a decision to release all of them on SoundCloud, for free. "If we can get these beautiful sound recordings out and let people in the world listen to them, maybe we can start protecting what we've got left." These recordings have been used in more than 150 films and numerous nature documentaries. As a result of his generosity, they'll be available in perpetuity.

- Bridging organization Living Room Conversations offers more than one hundred free conversation guides and other resources about broaching difficult subjects (abortion, for example) and reaching mutual understanding. They also run free online training.

- US hip-hop duo Run the Jewels made the album *RTJ4* "free for anyone who wants some music." To quote rapper El-P, the decision was "the only way I really know how to contribute to the human struggle and experience beyond just trying to be kind and aware and grow."

- The iconic French photographer Yann Arthus-Bertrand captivated imaginations with his remarkable photographs of the earth taken from hot-air balloons. He went on to make the deeply inspirational movies *Home, Human,* and *Woman,* each costing millions of dollars. His price for distributing them? Zero dollars. They're his gift to humanity, and are available for free on YouTube and elsewhere. And they have touched people deeply. YouTuber @joejoezidane, one of seven million people to watch the English version of *Human* on YouTube, said: "This is by far, the most powerful and overwhelming documentary that I have seen in my entire life."

I'm not arguing that everything offered for free online is a case of generosity. Just that where there is genuine generous intent, the Internet can multiply it a thousandfold.

But what about the growing numbers of artists, musicians, film-makers, influencers, and social media stars who count on the Internet for their income? I can imagine them reading this and thinking: *Not fair! You're expecting me to give away my best work without compensation? Then how will I live?*

These are legitimate concerns, and I'm certainly not saying that all that can be given away should be given away. Today's easy distribution of all forms of digital content has been at best a mixed blessing to many creative professionals. Take photographers. It used to be that a large percentage of the world's most viewed photographs were taken by professionals and distributed via newspapers, magazines, and television. But since the arrival of smartphones, the quantity of photographs taken and shared has increased by many orders of magnitude. Social media views of photos are in aggregate vastly greater than traditional media views. Many magazines and newspapers have been put out of business. And photographers have had to scramble to find new ways to get paid. For them, it is probably galling to think of the widespread sharing of photos as generous in any way, shape, or form.

Likewise, the ability for musicians to make money online is incredibly constrained. The deals negotiated by the record labels with companies like Spotify mean that there may need to be as many as 2,500 listens to a musician's music for them to earn a single dollar. The Internet has allowed far more music to be heard by far more people than ever before in history, but it's harder than ever to make a living providing that music.

Many writers, artists, and filmmakers may feel the same way. And the rapidly escalating power of generative AI just makes things worse.

But if the business models of the Internet are unkind to creators, perhaps generosity itself can play a role in fixing this. Could we nurture a fledgling gift economy to support our creatives? Sites like Patreon specifically allow people to provide financial support to their favorite artists and creators. And a growing number of platforms that allow distribution of content are making it possible for users to tip the creators they like most.

There's room to push this thinking a lot further. On March 23, 2020, the UK went into Covid-related lockdown. For a large proportion of the population, there was suddenly no work and no income. Fewer were harder hit than self-employed artists. Many had been living on very thin margins before the pandemic. When the galleries shut and exhibitions costing years of work were instantly canceled, many were plunged into poverty.

Artist and social entrepreneur Matthew Burrows knew he needed to do something—and quickly—to help himself and his friends. "I've got to build something that spreads like the virus does, but it spreads something that can help people," he thought. A student of anthropology, he took great inspiration from generous cultures of the premodern world. Perhaps he could use ancient principles of gift culture and mutual aid to help some artists survive.

Taking to Instagram, he created the #ArtistSupportPledge, a social media movement with a few basic rules:

- Post images of your work on Instagram with the hashtag #ArtistSupportPledge.
- Charge no more than £200 (or its equivalent) for any work.
- Once you have made sales worth at least £1,000, fulfill the pledge by buying another artist's work for £200.
- If in doubt, act in a spirit of generosity, that's all that matters.

These rules effectively equipped his fellow artists with a new platform that would connect them with their supporters and offer sustenance. Suddenly it was easier for them to sell their work and easier for them to support one another.

Burrows expected the #ArtistSupportPledge to benefit just a small circle of his friends based in the London area. But when a network that empowers people reaches a certain critical mass, it can take off with a life of its own. The pledge went viral on Instagram, with professional and amateur artists from all over the world buying one another's work, further supported by others inspired by the project. By the end of the pandemic, the generous culture of the #ArtistSupportPledge had raised an astonishing £70 million for artists.

My brilliant research assistant Kate Honey, who helped track down many of the stories in this book, spoke with Matthew. "ASP is fueled by generosity," he told her, "from what an artist offers for sale at a capped or discounted price—which includes all artists, regardless of prestige, experience, or reputation—to their pledge to share 20 percent of sales with peers and colleagues. Generosity can be seen in the way that buyers extend trust in the artist, engaging directly to purchase the work, without need for an intermediary."

What most inspired Burrows was how natural this ancient and modern "generous culture" seemed to be to artists. The #ArtistSupportPledge moderated itself and spread organically, with minimal input from Burrows. "If you start talking about kindness, people think you're crazy, or you've lost it. When the #ArtistSupportPledge went global, what was really exciting was that for the first time in my career I could talk about kindness like it wasn't something that was ridiculous or stupid or soft. Kindness is a tough, effective response to the world."

How far could this go? Can we imagine a shift from a world of relatively scarce creative content controlled and paid for by a few gatekeepers to a world of abundant creativity of all kinds paid for by the generous responses of the receivers of that content?

To take the example of Patreon, as of early 2023, it had distributed a total of $3.5 billion to 250,000 different creators—an average of about $14,000 each. Now, that's over several years and so—except in a few cases—it's nowhere near yet providing a full, fair income to artists. But it does show some promise for what could be.

What's clear is that we're in a transition period, and my advice to creators, professional and otherwise, would be: Don't fight it, try to get ahead of it. That is to say, try embracing generosity as part of your distribution strategy. That might mean, for example, freely giving away the most awesome thing you can create, while also giving people a chance to respond generously in turn. (This could be as simple as creating your Patreon account and making clear that you're dependent on people's support to make a living.)

And my advice to the rest of us, the lucky recipients of an unprecedented torrent of amazingness, is to think of all this through a generosity lens. How lucky are we that so many people out there are willing to share their best work, and that we can get instant access to it? This has never happened before in history. We should respond in kind. Take the effort to identify those who have most moved, inspired, informed, or taught you—and support them as generously as you can in whatever manner would be most meaningful to them.

We may collectively be in the process of creating a rich and varied gift economy that in time could grow to match or even exceed today's transactional economy. One day we may look back on the limited strictures of transactional creativity and thank our lucky stars that it's no longer how things get done.

And in the meantime, any creative who charges a subscription, participates in advertising or sponsorship revenue, or creates a pay wall, because that's what they need to do for the moment, that is just fine too. We may well end up with a mixed model for a very long time. Make that the bedrock of your living, but maybe still allow time for the occasional generosity experiment where you try giving away something in a surprising manner. You could end up delighted by what happens in response.

3. Everyone Is Watching

Reputation has always been a crucial currency for humans. Much of our effectiveness and much of our happiness depend on what others think of us.

For most of human history, people's reputations were shaped by the small group they lived with. Today a single piece of content can enter the minds of thousands or even millions of people within a few hours, carrying with it the reputation of its creator. That's a mind-boggling development. It has the potential to create unlimited upside for acts perceived as good and unlimited downside for those that aren't.

Reputation has always been the secret enforcer of behavior. In the small communities of our ancestors, no one could afford to earn a reputation for being greedy or untrustworthy. That would quickly result in social isolation and a short, sad life.

As societies grew and people began to live in larger, more anonymous towns and cities, it became easier to hide some behaviors, and some people could be less dependent on the approval of others. Grifters, con artists, and snake-oil salesmen roamed from small town to small town without consequence. Selfishness and crime could sometimes be indulged in without anyone having to pay the ultimate social price.

But the unstoppable increase in the ways in which we are connected has changed the rules once again. Hundreds of Internet services are recording and monitoring our reputations in different ways. People on the other side of the planet can tell someone else about something we've written or created. Greater transparency raises the risks for bad behavior and the rewards for doing things right. Now it's not just your village that knows. It's the whole world.

After giving away its talks, TED blossomed out of nowhere, because the Internet gave it a global reputation. Few people had heard of TED in 2006. But within a couple of years, millions were hooked. And they quickly spread the word.

Gifts have always carried with them the likelihood of payback in the form of enhanced reputation. And we're in an age when that reputation can spread indefinitely.

But is that always good? For many of us, the thought that someone on the other side of the world, or in a powerful corporation, or in a government agency, can see what we're doing is the stuff of nightmares. Surely, you may feel, this is exactly what's wrong with the Internet. We don't need more reputational spread; we need *privacy*.

Certainly when knowledge of someone's actions can spread across the world, there can be both good and bad consequences. A single kind act can transform how someone is regarded. When billionaire Robert Smith announced during his commencement speech at Morehouse College in 2019 that he was paying off the student loan debts of the entire graduating class, the story exploded on social media and garnered headlines around the world. His generosity was lauded in hundreds of media posts and he was named by Bloomberg as one of the fifty people who defined the year. If Smith had been try-ing to buy that kind of publicity, it would have cost far more than the money he pledged.

Yet it works the other way too. Back in 2014, marketing profes-sional Justine Sacco hit Send on a single misguided tweet just before she took off on a flight from the United States to South Africa. It was forwarded to a gossip site and went viral in the ugliest way. While she was in the air, tens of thousands of judgmental responses poured in from all over the world. By the time she landed she had already been fired. You can't watch Jon Ronson's TED Talk about that story with-out your heart pumping with the stress of it. It took her years to get her life back on track.

Others have fared worse still. Online shaming can drive people to suicide. And governments and corporations can exploit their knowl-edge of our actions to manipulate us.

But uncomfortable though it may be, I'd like to argue that overall the growing importance of reputation on the Internet is a force for good.

A few years ago, I heard a tale that gripped me. There was a night-time break-in at a beautiful old house packed with exotic, valuable objects. The burglar gasped in awe as he carefully guided his flash-light over the giant oil paintings on the wall and the polished antique furniture shrouded with expensive silks. But before he could pick anything up, he was stopped in his tracks by a loud voice above his head.

"Jesus is watching you."

Fighting to stay calm, he turned the flashlight upward . . . and then guffawed in relief. "Ha! You're just a parrot. Bless you, Jesus."

"Actually, my name's Polly. Jesus is the rottweiler standing behind you."

I tell this story because I spent the first twenty-five years of my life believing that Jesus was indeed watching me. And, even though I now think that's unlikely to have been true, that belief probably made me a better person. For example, it probably made me hesitate before lying or cheating. And on occasion it probably nudged me to try to be kinder than I otherwise might have been.

Human minds are weird things. We're actually quite fragile. We find it hard to navigate the complicated social world we live in. We find it challenging to take full account of the needs of others. Arguably, we need all the help we can get.

Which is why religions—and parents—have invented a remarkably creative set of stories to motivate us to do the right thing. Take Santa Claus, for example. I have it on good authority that he's not only making a list, he's checking it twice. He will definitely find out if you're naughty or nice. Santa Claus is watching you.

And he's not the only one. Many of us grew up with the idea of an all-knowing God constantly monitoring our behavior. Did that change how we behaved? It surely did.

The philosopher Alain de Botton, who's an atheist, gave a TED Talk arguing that we should be wary of throwing out all the accoutrements of religion, even if we no longer believe its fundamental stories. Isn't it odd, for example, that pretty much every religion recommends that its followers meet at least weekly to be reminded of their religious and moral duties? Perhaps humans need those regular nudges to increase their chances of doing the right thing.

We talk in awe of the sacrifices made by "the greatest generation" in order to survive a decade of the Depression and win the Second World War. But we forget, perhaps, that every week, for most of their lives, they assembled in churches, synagogues, and mosques to recommit to causes bigger than they were. Now that we've let much of that go—certainly in most Western nations—is it a surprise that civic duty is also in decline?

Perhaps humans are at their best when their decision-making calculus includes just a little bit of caution at the prospect of being caught doing something bad. I'm all for using the tools of encouragement and inspiration as juicy carrots to nudge people toward the right actions. But if we use only positive incentives, I'm not sure all of us—when times are hardest, when we're under pressure, when we have too many commitments or demands to juggle—would find the resolve to be our best selves.

All of which is to say that Internet-fueled reputation may have a meaningful role to play in our futures. Jesus may or may not be watching us. But the Internet certainly is.

Now, I am 100 percent in favor of limiting the surveillance that governments and companies are tempted to indulge in. And I'm alarmed by the excesses of cancel culture. If the whole world is now a village, please let's not arm the villagers with pitchforks. What I'm arguing for is a position with a dash of nuance: one that says we can view the transparency that spreads our reputations as an overall force for good while still seeking to avoid abusing it.

In the years to come, I suspect that more and more aspects of our lives are going to be tracked and measured. We can fight it. Or we can embrace the good side of it and plan for a future in which our reputations are going to matter ever more.

Maybe this will actually feel good. Certainly it's joyful to hear from people online who may have heard about something you've done and want to thank you for it. But the other side of the coin—the fear of disapproval—can also benefit us. It's okay for us sometimes to pause and wonder if some act we're contemplating will be well received by others.

So that's my takeaway. We've entered an era in which, increasingly, our mantra should be: *Act as if everyone is watching.* Because they may well be. It can be uncomfortable. And I appreciate that not everyone is ready to welcome this aspect of our connected age. But often discomfort is a proxy for progress. You will gain extra motivation from it to be your best self. And if, perchance, you do something great, word of it may spread far and wide, opening doors you can scarcely imagine.

The New Logic of Generosity

So let's put those three things together.

- Nonmaterial things are playing an ever more important role in our lives.
- It's easily possible to give them away on an unlimited scale.
- Everyone is watching, which means that giving offers unlimited impact on the biggest currency of our age: reputation.

This combination makes clear why individuals and organizations may want to dial up the role generosity could play in their future. Together, these principles create both opportunity and obligation for us modern connected souls to think about generosity in a whole new way. We don't have to think of generosity as simply a noble act; we can start thinking of it as an essential *strategy*.

And yet we recoil at putting the words *generosity* and *strategy* together. Generosity is supposed to be heartfelt, not calculated. How can we reconcile this?

3

IMPERFECT GENEROSITY

*Why we should welcome multiple
motivations for giving*

t is almost impossible for someone today to act generously without
getting sniped at. Naysayers abound.

That beautiful new initiative that got funded? *The money donated was tarnished.*

That video that drew millions of eyes to a terrible problem? *Well,
it didn't change the system, did it?*

Someone devoted a year of their life to volunteering for a cause?
Shame on them. Why did they stop?

Is this just people making excuses to justify their own inaction? I
don't think so. It's often genuinely hard to know what to make of an
alleged generous act. Take a look at the opinions expressed by my
social media followers when I polled them on different versions of
the same story.

Notably, some people were willing to count the act as generous in

Francis gives $5,000 to a charity. It pays for vital surgery that restores the sight of a child.

- **Generous 97%**
- Not Generous 3%

Add this context: Francis is a billionaire.

- **Generous 69%**
- Not Generous 31%

Francis earned the money from a business whose employees have to put up with horrendous working conditions.

- **Generous 51%**
- Not Generous 49%

RESET. Francis gives $5,000 to a charity. It pays for vital surgery that restores the sight of a child. Francis never tells a soul about this.

- **Generous 99%**
- Not Generous 1%

Francis films the entire process for a YouTube channel, in a manner designed to evoke powerful emotions. The video gets five million views.

- **Generous 56%**
- Not Generous 44%

Now, factor in this additional detail: At least one hundred commenters on the YouTube page say they're inspired and will now also support restoration of sight.

- **Generous 81%**
- Not Generous 19%

RESET. Francis gives $5,000 to a charity. It pays for vital surgery that restores the sight of a child. Tragically, the eye becomes infected, and the child dies a week later.

- **Generous 97%**
- Not Generous 3%

Francis knew that the charity had often been criticized for using unqualified medical staff.

- Generous 39%
- **Not Generous 61%**

RESET. Francis gives $5,000 to a charity. It pays for vital surgery that restores the sight of a child. The child had been blinded when she swerved on her bike and was hit by Francis's car.

- Generous 49%
- **Not Generous 51%**

The car was driving at sixty mph in a thirty mph residential zone.

- Generous 22%
- **Not Generous 78%**

every single case. As one commenter, Charles Scott, put it: "If you freely give any amount of your own money to help someone in need without any expectation of something in return, then you are generous. Your relative wealth or how you made your money may speak to your moral virtue, but I don't think it diminishes an act of generosity." And sometimes context that seemed damaging could be impacted by more knowledge, as when we discover that the YouTube video persuaded others to be generous.

In general, my followers seemed to be most impacted by any sign that someone's intent might be impure. In fact, they cared much more about that than they did about the actual result of the gift. Where the surgery failed through no apparent fault of the giver, the act was viewed as just as generous as when it succeeded. This suggests that when people think about generosity, they're usually not evaluating the long-term results; they're simply evaluating the intent of the giver. Was this a hard thing for them to do or was it a trivial thing? Was it done with pure sincerity or were there mixed motives?

Think about that for a moment. Can it really be right that we care more about intent than results? If we want to think of generosity as just some kind of moral test of character, then I guess that makes sense. But if you believe, as I do, that our entire future depends on how effectively we use our generosity, then we may need to reset our own assumptions.

Kant Can't Be Right

The idea that generosity is all about pure *intent* is part of a long line of religious and philosophical thinking. The German philosopher

Immanuel Kant taught that an act had moral worth *only* if it was performed out of a sense of duty. If you got any other benefit from it, then it was a form of selfishness.

But based on what we know today of human psychology, it's hard to justify this position. Every human decision is made for *some* kind of benefit, even if it's simply satisfying the call of conscience. Satisfying that call scratches an itch. In some sense, it feels good. Otherwise, we wouldn't do it. To quote Joey from *Friends,* "There is no unselfish good deed."

As a philosophy student, I spent hours agonizing over this point. In a nutshell: How could I *ever* be a good person if being good felt good? That would mean that being good was in some sense being selfish, which was a contradiction. But if being good *didn't* bring some kind of satisfaction with it, how would I ever find the motivation to be good? How would anyone?

With all due apologies to Kant, I think it's time to let go of this confusing restriction. It's okay for people to have multiple reasons or good feelings behind their acts of giving. This sets us free to focus more on the *effectiveness* of giving than the nuances of the motivation behind it. If the giving results in lives being saved or improved, I don't mind that the giver also gets joy out of it. Or that the giver is secretly hoping the act will help her long-term reputation. In fact, I think those motivations can be celebrated. Because they open the door to persuading more people to be generous.

In short, I think we should welcome a world where generosity can be thought of as a conscious *strategy* motivated by multiple factors. *Yes,* I want to address someone else's need. *Yes,* I want to do the right thing and feel good about myself. *Yes,* I want to give in a way that could trigger others to respond in kind. *Yes,* I'm excited that all this could ultimately help my reputation. Once we collectively accept that all this is okay, it will remove so much of the nitpicking and hypocrisy that conversations about generosity often entail.

Now, there's still a line that can be crossed where seeming acts of generosity are truly cynical. The corporation that is simply greenwashing. Or the rapacious businessman trying to redeem himself by boasting about his charitable gifts. Or, in the case above, when Francis had caused the problem in the first place through his own reckless driving.

I accept that those probably don't count as examples of generosity. But even in instances like those, we should be cautious about rushing to judgment. None of us can see inside someone else's head. We often can't be sure what someone's motivation is, even our own. Therefore I believe in adopting the following principle: Whenever possible, *give someone the benefit of the doubt*. That itself is a meaningful act of generosity. A world in which everyone takes a cynical view of others' motivations quickly turns dark.

So if someone gives money to a local school, and then gets their name in the newspaper, just possibly it was a selfish act done purely for self-promotion. But if we assume that, we ourselves are not being generous. Much better is to imagine that at least part of the motivation was a genuine desire to see kids at the school do better. (For what it's worth, the science suggests that over the long term gratitude is a far stronger motivator of generosity than a conscious desire for reputation.)

Likewise, it's not constructive to criticize someone's generosity just because you think it didn't go far enough. Systemic change, or even just creating a major impact on a given problem, is hard, and pretty much every gift ever given probably could have been improved in some way, even if just by increasing its amount. If we focus on the imperfections rather than the positive good achieved, we're falling into the trap of letting the perfect be the enemy of the good. It's hard to give things away. We should be encouraging each other, not finding reasons to tear each other down. First encourage, *then* maybe have a conversation about how things could have been even better. And be ready to offer your own contribution.

To summarize, we need not discount the generosity of others just because they may have additional motives for doing what they do. There are *always* additional motives. A generosity strategy is a good thing. And there is no such thing as "perfect" generosity. Unless it's clear that an act was truly cynical, we should give people the benefit of the doubt and celebrate their kindness.

What About Billionaires?

Can we adopt this mindset when it comes to supposed acts of generosity by the ultra-rich? It's certainly harder. Billionaires who make philanthropic gifts are often accused of simply seeking to buy public approval. Or, worse, seeking to shore up the broken system that made them wealthy in the first place.

The most extreme version of this criticism says that it's not the role of private citizens to try to solve our societal problems. This is the government's task. We should all simply campaign for a tax system that takes a much bigger share from the wealthy, to the point where it's impossible even to become a billionaire.

I have a lot of sympathy with these arguments. Growing inequality is indeed a huge problem. The fact that CEOs in America make about three hundred times the median pay of their workers (as opposed to twenty times fifty years ago) just seems horribly wrong. And it is shocking that the world's 2,700 billionaires have more wealth than the 120 poorest countries combined. Anyone who was trying to design a global system from a blank sheet of paper would never argue that something like this should be the goal.

What's more, there definitely are billionaires who have used their philanthropy cynically. And even when that isn't the case, it's infuriating that *they* should get to decide what change looks like. In a thriving democracy, key decisions about our lives should be made with everyone's engagement. And most should be funded through the public purse, via taxation, in which the rich pay much higher taxes.

I support the idea of more progressive taxation. But here's the problem: Best-case scenario, it's going to take years. Part of the reason for that is, yes, the rich can use their wealth to influence political decisions. But there's a more potent reason why this will be hard. The wealthy are mobile. They can choose to up and move to another country. Taxes, by and large, are not mobile. They are levied by national governments. No nation can afford to raise taxes to the point where it scares off its wealthiest citizens.

In the meantime, private capital will continue to pile up in ever greater amounts. This is happening for several reasons. As the French economist Thomas Piketty has documented, people with wealth can achieve inflation-adjusted investment gains of 5 percent or more annually, which is greater than most countries' rate of economic growth. So on average they will gain wealth relative to a median citizen.

And there's an even more fundamental cause of rising inequality: the world's growing connectedness. Fifty years ago, if you started a business, it would likely take decades before you could reach your first million customers. Today, there are examples of companies reaching one *billion* customers in just a few years. Facebook, Google, and Amazon would be three examples. For Internet-based businesses, the entire world lies just a click away. Even without questionable business practices, it's easy to see how the founders of these companies could have become absurdly wealthy.

So what are we to say to billionaires? That they should just hang on to their wealth while we try to figure out how to tax the heck out of them? This would effectively waste one of the world's biggest resources. If that had been our stance these past couple of decades, global efforts at tackling polio, trachoma, child mortality, and a host of other causes would have been crippled. *Forbes* magazine estimates that the combined wealth of the world's billionaires is more than $12 trillion. That is enough money, as we'll see, to make a giant impact on many of the world's biggest problems. It's crazy to think that instead of attempting those things, the money should just sit there, accumulating another 5 to 10 percent every year.

Here's a different idea. Why not be a little more strategic? While we're working on the reforms that may or may not one day usher in a fairer world, why don't we try to persuade the world's billionaires to triple down on their philanthropic efforts, but to do so in a way that maximizes the public good? The problem isn't too much philanthropy by rich people, it's *too little*. According to calculations by *Forbes,* the total known lifetime donations from the majority of billionaires are less than 5 percent of their current net worth. We shouldn't be telling them that their philanthropy is a terrible idea. We should be urging them to do a lot more, and engaging in a conversation about what type of spending would be most valuable.

I suspect many billionaires would like to do that. In fact, I know this to be true. As I'll describe in chapter 12, for several years now, I have overseen an initiative called The Audacious Project. The purpose of that initiative is to find powerful philanthropic projects that are in the interests of us all, and then persuade donors to support them. Many of those donors are indeed billionaires, and I know from numerous personal conversations how important it is to them to try to do philanthropy the right way.

If we let go of our instinct to view generosity through a perfection filter, we could find a healthier, more productive dialogue. We could give one another, rich and poor, the benefit of the doubt and see if we can work on this together. Our goal isn't to exhibit perfect virtue. It's to try to make things better. And that will happen one step at a time, with all of us acknowledging one another's efforts, and encouraging each other to find even better ways to give.

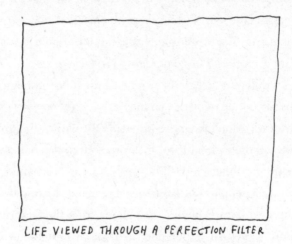

LIFE VIEWED THROUGH A PERFECTION FILTER

But how do we find the motivation to be generous in the first place? With so many other demands on our lives, isn't it unnatural and unreasonable to expect us to look beyond ourselves?

This is a key question. One of the joys of running TED has been getting to know some of the world's leading psychologists and evolutionary biologists. Let me share what I've learned from their talks, from their books, and from numerous personal conversations. I've found them to be both fascinating and exhilarating.

SECRET SUPERPOWERS

The powerful seeds of generosity inside every human

n my twenties, when I was slowly letting go of my religious beliefs, one key question gave me pause. Without God in my life, what reason would I ever have to try to do the right thing? To be kind to people? To be anything other than selfish?

I had always thought that conscience had been created by God as an essential moral compass. If God didn't exist, what possible argument could *anyone* make that sometimes sacrifices should be made for the common good? Weren't we ultimately then just out for our own interests? Isn't that what secular biology taught? That we were evolved animals engaged in a battle for survival, like every other creature?

But when I started connecting with leading thinkers outside religion, I came to understand that this wasn't what modern evolutionary biology taught at all. Rather than being hardwired purely for selfishness, I learned that evolution could also create creatures with strong desires to behave in selfless ways. Those instincts are what make infectious generosity possible.

The Girl and the Carpenter

On the evening of February 5, 2022, a thirty-seven-year-old carpenter named Mohammed Mehboob stood at a railroad crossing in Bhopal, India. On his way home from a prayer service at his mosque, he and his fellow travelers had stopped to let a freight train pass. A young girl wearing red stood nearby with her family, a knapsack on her shoulder. To their surprise, the train came to a halt. The girl and her family started across the tracks with the others—but suddenly the train started moving again. As people rushed forward to get clear, the girl got her foot stuck under the track and fell over. Amid cries of rising panic, Mohammed looked back and saw her sprawled on the tracks, the train rapidly approaching.

The girl tried to stand but fell again, frozen in fear. Mohammed raced back to the tracks. In a fraction of a second he saw it was too late to pull her clear of the oncoming train, so he dived onto the tracks and held her close to the ground, covering her head. Moments later the train roared over them, with carriage after carriage passing just inches above their heads. Finally, the immense battery of clanging metal gave way to sobs of relief. Both Mohammed and the girl were able to get up and walk away.

Mohammed continued home—he did not even stop to ask the girl her name. When a video of his lifesaving heroism went viral, he replied modestly that he had simply acted on instinct.

What kind of force would make someone act like this toward a stranger? It surely comes from the deepest part of a person. Such actions are sudden, spontaneous, and unutterably selfless and coura-geous, and as likely as not they come as a surprise to the person performing them as well as to everyone else.

Do you doubt this? Perhaps you feel that you could never ever do what Mohammed did. That may be true. But had you been there, you would certainly have *felt* something. Horrified at the advancing train, you'd have experienced an intense urge to protect that poor girl. Perhaps that urge would have been offset by a fervent desire not to risk your life. But the very fact that it was there at all is remarkable.

Try this thought experiment. You are walking home and you no-tice that same girl sitting on a bench at the side of the road. She has covered her head with her arms. She is shaking in fear. It's not clear why. But you can see she is in deep distress. There is no one else around. Now what do you do?

This time a greater proportion of us would act. We might at least go over and ask her if she's okay. But still, not all of us would. The instinct for generosity is always offset, to a lesser or greater extent, by another instinct called loss aversion. We simply don't want to give up what we have, and that includes giving up our current level of com-fort. Perhaps you are late for an important dinner. Perhaps you worry that if you go and sit down next to her you may get pulled into some-thing you don't want to get pulled into. Perhaps you think she's bait for some kind of criminal attack on you. But even if the loss aversion ultimately wins out, I guarantee you will have felt a powerful urge to help that girl. That feeling is the raw desire wired into every human that we should look out for one another.

Why should that feeling even be there at all? We're biological en-tities trying to survive. Why should we be distracted by risky feelings that could cause us to act in someone else's interests rather than our own?

How Selfish Genes Can Make Unselfish People

We sometimes think of our evolutionary history as a lineage of life-forms in bloody competition with each other: "Nature, red in tooth and claw," as Alfred Lord Tennyson put it. But there are many ways to compete. It turns out that one of the best ways for a group of animals to survive and thrive is to become instinctively *un*selfish.

Many animals have developed such instincts: ants, dolphins, elephants, dogs, and bonobos, to name a few. And humans too. There are many ways these instincts could have developed. As the cognitive scientist Steven Pinker put it to me: "All you need is the reality that an organism can confer a large benefit to another at a small cost to itself, that these roles can reverse, and that the members of an intelligent and social species can take advantage of these asymmetries."

In other words, groups that live with each other, and that have the mental sophistication to remember how each member of the group behaves over multiple interactions, will readily adapt a form of reciprocal generosity. *I have some food to spare at this moment, so I can share some with you. It won't necessarily cost me much, but it could save your life. You will remember what I did, and one day you will share your food with me. We all benefit.*

For this to realize its full potential, humans needed over time to build a suite of essential emotional adaptations, including sympathy for those in need, gratitude for those who have helped, anger at those who cheat and never give back, and guilt at not doing enough. It's these emotions acting in concert that drive our instincts for generosity and ensure that they're employed frequently, fairly, and effectively. And the genes that build these emotions have thereby constructed a remarkable strategy for themselves to survive and thrive and be passed on. Indeed, our ancestors passed them on to us.

In-groups and Out-groups

These emotions were fine-tuned for how humans lived as hunter-gatherers in small groups of maybe 150 individuals, and as a consequence they don't necessarily extend beyond members of our tribe. Indeed, psychological research confirms that most of us naturally categorize people into "in-groups" and "out-groups." Typically, the former are people we grew up with or who are part of our community. Our empathetic instincts are dialed up much more strongly for those in our in-group. For others who are perceived as outsiders, we may well initially react with indifference, suspicion, or even cruelty.

But here's the exciting thing. Social science experiments have shown that the boundary between in-group and out-group is malleable. It is not indelibly linked to characteristics such as skin color, religion, geography, or accent. For example, in one study, giving a diverse group of individuals a single team name, or simply seating them together, rapidly created in-group loyalty.

In other studies, being told someone's story transforms how people think about that person. When you see that another human being carries the same fears, hopes, and dreams that you do, it makes it utterly natural to treat them the same way as anyone else in your in-group. The widespread reading of novels is credited with helping expand people's circle of empathy, and there have been similar effects from watching movies and TV shows.

Back in 2008, TED helped the award-winning filmmaker Jehane Noujaim create a day (Pangea Day) in which a million people around the world spent four hours watching films that shared powerful stories told in the voices of those from many different countries. The idea was that by putting ourselves in each other's shoes, we would be drawn closer. And that was certainly the reported experience of those who participated. Winnet Murahwa, a student at a school in Hawaii who watched with her classmates, commented, "I couldn't take my eyes off the screen. It was a spiritual experience for me." Her classmate April Sanchez concurred: "I felt more human knowing that there were people around the world like me going through the same struggles."

So we humans evolved instincts that power generosity within our in-group. But we have the ability to expand that in-group without limit. This is promising! And now we turn to another instinct that plays a key role in extending the reach of our generosity.

The Urge to Respond

Humans are famous for reciprocating all manner of social behaviors. Be playful with me, I'll be playful with you. Be mean to me, and you better watch out.

The natural desire to respond in kind is a core part of our generosity engine. Numerous social experiments have demonstrated this, including a major new experiment we'll dive into in the next chapter. If people are kind to us, we instinctively respond in the same spirit, in both our future actions toward them and in our actions toward others. This is regardless of whether we are already part of their in-group. Indeed, this urge to respond is a natural way of expanding in-groups.

I've tested this response instinct on several occasions and have always been amazed at the results. For example, I was invited to give a talk back at the school I attended in Bath, England. At the start of the talk I handed out my phone to the group of graduating students in the front rows (most of them aged seventeen or eighteen) and invited them to enter their email addresses if they wanted to take part in a stressful, time-consuming experiment that would nonetheless reveal something important about each of them.

Thirteen students were brave enough to enter their emails. At the end of the talk, somewhat to the shock of their parents and the teaching staff, I told them I was sending each of them £1,000 to spend as they wished in the coming month, with only one condition: that they report back later on what they spent it on.

The headmaster's fears of drug-fueled parties proved groundless. Almost all the students spent the money on outside causes they supported. Two years later, the experience was still meaningful to them.

For example, one student, Archie Griffiths, donated his gift to a charity called CALM, which was working to prevent suicide in men. But his research into its work also inspired him to become a crisis volunteer. He told me: "It's shown me that one person's effort can lead to the saving of lives."

Another, Ophelia Fellhauer, divided her money between an LGBT organization and a group in Malawi empowering girls. She wrote: "I got to spend time with the people the money was going to, and see the impact our support was having on their lives. It is the most incredible and rewarding feeling, and an experience I will never forget. This experiment was one of the most inspiring and motivating experiences of my school career."

Were their decisions influenced by the fact that they had to reveal later what the money was spent on? Was this basically a form of virtue signaling? In part, no doubt it was. But consider these two angles: (1) they could still easily have spent it on, say, needs for their first year in university or some other investment in their future, and (2) the fact that they may have cared about the reputational impact of their choices puts them in exactly the same position as almost everyone giving things away in our ever-more transparent world. Reputation matters, and it's fantastic that it can encourage generosity. We should celebrate these long-term self-interest motivations.

There's another way in which generosity can become naturally infectious. Even if you're not the recipient of generosity, simply seeing someone else be generous can inspire you to give. This is true to some extent for all human traits. We're massively influenced by one another. The work of Nicholas Christakis and others has shown that behaviors spread dramatically through human networks. If our circle of friends—and their friends—exhibit distinctive behaviors, we may well adopt those behaviors ourselves. But in the case of generosity the effect is amplified by what social psychologist Jonathan Haidt calls "moral elevation." When we witness a good act on the part of someone else to a third party, it has an actual physical effect on us— a warm feeling of uplift that inspires us to want to follow suit, thereby creating the potential for a chain reaction of kindness.

There's a YouTube video called Kindness Boomerang from the group Life Vest Inside that depicts this type of chain reaction. It's a street scene in which one kind event inspires a sequence of others. Interestingly, just the act of watching that video seems to have created that same feeling of uplift—the video has more than thirty million views, and hundreds of thousands of appreciative comments saying things like "I used to watch this video all the time in the car on the way to school and I really think it shaped me as a person. It inspired me to commit many acts of kindness. . . ."

So think about that. You don't need to see a generous act in the real world. Simply watching it on video can be enough to trigger a moral elevation response. Then remember that we're in a world where videos can be freely shared with an unlimited number of people. That's promising, no?

Beyond Empathy

So. We're built to be generous, and to respond to generosity whether as recipients or just as witnesses. These are beautiful, underreported facts. Put them together and it's clear how chain reactions of generous behavior can take off. But we need to be mindful of something. Because although our instincts for generosity run deep, they don't always push us in exactly the right direction. They were built for a world where we lived in small communities. They are most dialed up when we perceive an individual in pain or at risk. They aren't a perfect guide to imagining how best to help larger groups of people or, indeed, the planet as a whole.

Psychologist Paul Bloom has argued that too much reliance on just our empathetic instincts can lead to us focusing only on the needs of individuals who we feel are part of our in-group, and ignoring the broader interests of society. It can also cause us to care more about individuals than to help out larger numbers. You can't *see* larger groups. It's no accident that charities that use a picture of a single suffering child can raise money more easily than those arguing to save the lives of millions.

Our Reflective Selves Versus Our Lizard Brains

The answer here is not to rely on our instincts but to engage our reflective minds. In my religious upbringing, I was taught that life was a battle between our inner demons and our divinity. The details may have been wrong, but there's a modern version of that story that I think is fundamental to understanding ourselves. Today, so often the key mental battles we must deal with are between our *instinctive selves* and our *reflective selves*. And those are fundamentally two different mental systems, as has been beautifully articulated by the great psychologist Daniel Kahneman in his book *Thinking, Fast and Slow.*

Our instinctive self is what he calls System 1 thinking, "a machine for jumping to conclusions." It operates quickly, so quickly we're often unconscious of its actions. It has instant control over our muscles and can make us flee from danger. But it can also be accompanied by intense basic emotions: fear, lust, anger, greed. I'll sometimes use the term "lizard brain" to describe this part of us. I don't mean to suggest that there's a literal inner lizard; it's just a powerful shorthand for our instinctive selves.

Unlike the demons of my youth, our lizard brains bring us many key benefits, offering our lives efficient, fast, unconscious decision-making; lots of excitement; lots of pleasure; and—yes—the core instincts that drive our generosity. But our lizard brains can also get us into deep trouble. Every tale of violence, addiction, or thoughtless cruelty has lizard brain activity at its heart. And when it comes to generosity, our base instincts can take us only so far.

Happily, it's just part of who we are. Uniquely among animals, we have evolved a giant prefrontal cortex. Yes, part of this is used to further enhance our instinctual activities. But it has also allowed us to have a reflective self, our voice of wisdom and oversight, what Kahneman labeled as System 2 thinking. This is the part of us that tells stories about who we are and who we want to be. It's the part of us that fights procrastination and thoughtfully tries to organize our lives to be productive and fulfilling and generous. If you ever find yourself asking, "How could I be my best self," that's your reflective self talking. When we're on our deathbeds asking whether we're proud of the lives we've lived, it's this reflective part of us that will be passing judgment.

So in pretty much every aspect of our lives, we have to engage our reflective minds and ask how best to channel our instincts. There's an analogy with diet. Our lizard brains crave sugar and fat whenever we can find it, making it all too easy today to have a diet dominated by junk food. To avoid that takes the engagement of our reflective selves. Likewise, when it comes to generosity, we need to consciously channel our sympathetic urges toward their best uses. Infectious generosity will be worthwhile only if it spreads acts that are wise as well as deeply felt.

Generosity Makes You Happier

There's one other element to our psychological model that could—if it were more widely known—act as a powerful driver of generosity.

It's a clear-cut finding in social science: *Generosity makes you happier.*

The polling firm Gallup surveys people in every country on many aspects of their lives, including their income, spending patterns, and happiness levels. An analysis of 230,000 respondents in 136 countries uncovered something spectacular. Those who reported donating money to charity the prior month were significantly happier than the rest. The size of the impact on their happiness was the same as if their annual income had *doubled*. Think about that for a minute. Most people believe that simply a 20 percent increase in their income would make a huge difference to their lives. But the Gallup data suggests they can have all the happiness that might come with that—and much more—simply by choosing to be generous.

Bear in mind that the data shows correlation, not necessarily causation. It may be that happy people are just more likely to donate money than unhappy people. But other studies reveal abundant evidence that there is indeed a causal link. In a typical experiment, subjects chosen at random who are invited to spend a sum of money on other people later report higher levels of happiness than those who spend it on themselves.

One of the leading scientific researchers of this topic is Professor Elizabeth Dunn of the University of British Columbia. In her TED Talk, she reported a study in which toddlers played the starring role, and even they showed greater markers for happiness when they gave away treats than when they received the treats themselves.

So the science seems to strongly support the wisdom attested to by many of history's most inspiring people: Generosity will bring you happiness. And yet I don't think very many people truly believe it. Many truths about happiness are commonplace. Love can make you happy. Beauty—whether in art or in nature—can make you happy.

Meaningful work can make you happy. Money—to an extent—can make you happy.

We know these things to be true and we spend huge amounts of effort pursuing them. But few people talk about the profound happiness that can come from giving.

One reason for this mismatch is that the happiness that comes from giving is often hidden from us in advance. When it comes to love or material success, our minds obsess. We crave those things, certain that they will bring us joy. With generosity, not so much. It's often swamped by loss aversion. *If I give this away, I lose it forever. Be careful!* It's only after we've acted that a feeling of joyful fulfillment comes over us.

This creates a dangerous asymmetry between our instincts to acquire and instincts to give. We lust after material gain, confident it will bring us joy. Indeed, our anticipatory radar *overstates* what's coming to us. The reality is that most material gains bring with them only short-term happiness. We then experience what's called hedonic adaptation. That is, we simply become accustomed to whatever we've got and start looking for the next thing we might aspire to.

Thus we are, in a sense, being manipulated by our own genes to be acquisition machines with insatiable appetites. You can understand why those genes could arise and thrive. They may be one key reason our species of strange, hairless apes relentlessly spread across the planet. But it doesn't mean the apes themselves got lasting happiness from it.

By contrast, it seems that generosity-sparked happiness is less susceptible to hedonic adaptation. In an experiment where subjects had the chance to spend money regularly either on themselves or on others, both groups initially reported satisfaction gains. But over time, the satisfaction level didn't fade for the second group.

We're odd things, we humans. The prospective happiness that shouts loudest doesn't deliver. The version that whispers oh so softly can last a lifetime.

Our whole lives, we'll face a conflict between the urge to accumulate versus the urge to give—to be a net taker or a net giver. Similar battles play out in countless other areas of human behavior: diet, anger, sex, procrastination. We owe it to ourselves to take a closer look at our instinctive behavior and use the more reflective parts of our minds to regulate it. We may discover that if we were to dial back our lust for more stuff in favor of regular acts of generosity, our long-term happiness levels would soar.

This Chinese proverb might be a teensy bit cynical about marriage, but otherwise says it all: *If you want happiness for an hour, take a nap. For a day, go fishing. For a month, get married. For a year, inherit a fortune. For a lifetime, help somebody else.*

Connecting the Dots

When you put the pieces together, it's easy to see how infectious generosity can become a potent force. There are two instincts deeply wired inside most humans: (1) the visceral desire to help others and (2) the automatic urge to respond to generosity in kind, whether as the recipient or as the witness. Those two instincts can light a fire that spreads generosity far and wide. But we need to control and direct that fire with reflective wisdom so that it can have maximum impact for good. Applying that wisdom may be challenging. Yet if we persist, our efforts won't be good just for the world; they will be good for us too. They will bring us a deep happiness that makes life worth living.

And now I think we have an answer to the question that used to haunt me. If we leave aside religious admonitions, what's the case for being generous? What do you say to people who would prefer just to look after themselves? Maybe this:

It's not always obvious, but generosity is a core part of who we are. Whether you think we were built by God or by evolution, we are wired to look out for each other. Our deepest fulfillment comes only when generosity is a fundamental part of our lives. No one can tell you what your specific obligations to your fellow humans are. But it's truly important that you find your own answers to that question. Your reputation, your long-term happiness, and the happiness of those around you all depend on it.

These truths about human nature hit home to me in the most powerful way when I was given a chance to help orchestrate a unique social experiment. Let me share with you the inside story of what happened.

THE MYSTERY EXPERIMENT

*Why strangers on the Internet were given
$10,000 and what happened next*

n 2019 a married couple in the TED community made an investment windfall. They wanted to respond to their good fortune by
giving away a good portion of it: $2 million. But rather than simply
support TED or another cause, they started to wonder if there might
be a more creative way to give away the money.

The idea they came up with was certainly creative. Audacious
even. They decided to give it away anonymously to strangers,
$10,000 at a time. And they wanted to collaborate with TED and
with social scientists to see if we could help amplify the impact of
these gifts.

Having already seen signs of generosity's power, I got excited at
the opportunity to help with this unlikely project and proposed a
dialed-up version of the experiment I had carried out at my school
described in the last chapter. Working with the psychologist Professor Elizabeth Dunn and her research team at the University of British

Columbia, we helped craft what came to be known as the Mystery Experiment.

Here's how it worked:

The Invitation

In December 2020, I put out a call on social media inviting people to apply to participate in an unusual research project. "It will be exciting, surprising, somewhat time-consuming, possibly stressful, but possibly also life-changing." No mention of money.

We tagged it #MysteryExperiment, and we ended up with a couple of thousand applicants, none of whom knew what they were signing up for. We selected a wide-ranging group of two hundred people from seven countries (Indonesia, Brazil, the UK, the US, Canada, Australia, and Kenya) and sent them a video sharing the good news: Each of them was to get a $10,000 gift from "an anonymous couple in the TED community" (transferred into a new PayPal account in their name). They could spend it *however they wanted*. The only major rules were:

- It had to be spent over the next three months.
- They had to report back to us on what they spent it on.

There was one other key twist. Half the group were encouraged to keep the news private. The other half were urged to share the news with their social media followers and to make occasional posts whenever they spent some of the money. (There was also a control group of one hundred who got only a small fee to fill in surveys. Unlucky for them, but they did add crucial scientific validity to the experiment.)

The Response

The results were genuinely exciting.

Just like the thirteen students in England, the vast majority of the two hundred recipients of the Mystery Experiment funds responded by simply giving away a significant portion of the money! On average, *only a third* of the money was spent on their own wants and needs. The rest was devoted to friends, family members, and outside causes. Even those who had the lowest incomes and for whom the sum was life-changing still, on average, gave away two-thirds of what they received.

This is convincing evidence against the so-called rational agent theory of economics, which posits that by and large people simply spend on themselves. Perhaps people will do that with money they have earned. But when they're recipients of someone else's generosity, it turns out they experience a strong desire to respond in kind.

One surprise is that there was no significant difference between those who could make their decisions privately and those who had to share their spending on social media. This implied that people were giving out of a natural instinct to reciprocate rather than out of the need for social approval from their online audience.

Their Stories

After the completion of the experiment, I reached out to some of the participants and was floored by what they told me.

Lydia Tarigan, a creative director based in Indonesia, spent almost none of the 140 million Indonesian rupiah she received on herself directly. Instead she gave 10 million rupiah to a co-worker to whom she felt grateful. And the same again to another. She gave 5 million to a colleague she knew less well, but who had recently been diagnosed with cancer. She donated millions of rupiah to the World Wildlife Fund and to flood victims and to a pet-rescue charity. She paid for health checkups for members of her family.

She told me, "When I learned I was selected, I screamed from the top of my lungs. Generosity is remarkable. It makes the recipient feel seen. It's like handing them their self-respect. It builds a bridge of connection between the giver and the recipient. So I wanted to make other people feel seen, just like how I had felt seen."

That instant desire to reciprocate was articulated beautifully by Claire Maxwell, from Canada. She said: "I often thought of the donors and my sense of wanting to make them proud. They took a tremendous financial risk and I wanted to do all that I could to pay this risk forward. I believe that I would have made different spending choices if I had won this same amount of money in a lottery. I never really felt that this was my money to spend—it was given to me by a family who thought beyond themselves. It was a privilege to share their gift with others."

A UK tech executive, Sarah Drinkwater, decided to give away the full $10,000—and then immediately had her resolve tested when an unexpected tax bill arrived the very next day for an even bigger sum. But she stuck with her plan and decided to make twenty mini-grants of $500 each, funding, for example, a pensioners' picnic, an artist's mural, and sensory toys for autistic children. She told me: "I walk past something I funded nearly every single day—the 3D-printed neighborhood mini–food bank, the bank of flowers outside a local school. So many of the recipients told me it was the public acknowledgment of their work that felt powerful, alongside the money. This project reminded me that things I hold true—community, care, joy, acting generously—are things others hold to be important too, and that I should believe in myself."

Kirk Citron, from the United States, said: "Instead of thinking of toys I might buy for myself, I quickly concluded: 'If the Mystery Experiment benefactor can give away $2 million, I can certainly give away $10,000.' I decided to 'pay it forward'—and, by giving it to Humanity Now (my chosen organization) as a matching grant, invited others to 'pay it forward' with me. Many joined in until, together, we were able to make a gift of $27,000. Generosity inspires generosity."

It's striking how many people specifically commented on the urge they felt to respond in kind to the donors' generosity. (To be clear, there was absolutely no formal obligation that they should do so. They were told they could spend the money however they chose. And there was no reason for them to think that they would ever hear from the anonymous donors again.) Thus, the experiment provided some of the most compelling scientific evidence yet of the robustness of people's inclination to respond to generosity with generosity of their own. Most prior experiments had been based on small gifts made to psychology students at universities. This was the biggest study done with a much larger sum involved and activated in multiple countries. In every single culture and at every single income level, people responded to generosity in kind.

The Happiness Angle

But there was another powerful scientific finding: further evidence of the strong correlation between generosity and happiness. We asked people to rate each big item of spending they completed according to how happy it made them feel in retrospect. The graph below indicates the results where 0.0 on the x-axis signals average happiness, while positive values signal more happiness than average. Donations brought significantly more pleasure than personal spending.

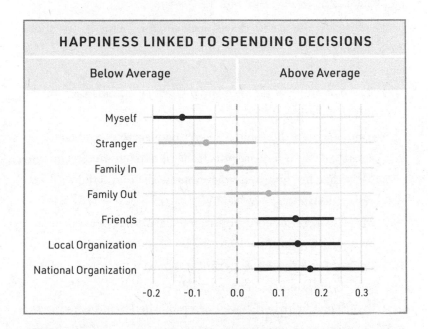

One of the most startling findings from the Mystery Experiment was described in a paper published in *Proceedings of the National Academy of Sciences* (*PNAS*) in late 2022. It estimated that the anonymous couple's donation had effectively created a more than 200x multiple of the amount of happiness that their $2 million could ever have given them personally. The paper has been cited as one of the most powerful arguments yet for the case for the rich to be generous with their wealth.

Let's dwell on that point for a moment, because it highlights the power of what can happen when generosity turns exponential. What if, instead of funding the experiment, the donor couple had decided to hold on to the money? Well, it would certainly have given them an extra measure of financial security, which is not nothing. It could have made two people and their immediate family a little more content for a few years.

But by going ahead with the experiment, they helped bring about the following:

- Two hundred people received a gift they'll remember for the rest of their lives.
- More than one thousand other individuals received benefits as a result of pay-it-forward gifts from the two hundred recipients.
- More than five hundred organizations all around the world received donations.
- More than one million people on social media got exposure (an average of six times each) to stories of generosity shared using the hashtag #MysteryExperiment. Some of them responded in kind. (One adopted an orangutan!)
- Two scientific papers have been published demonstrating the knock-on benefits of generosity at a scale never possible before.
- Happiness. A great deal of it. According to the *PNAS* paper, a two-hundred-fold multiplier of the happiness the couple themselves could receive from the money. (In reality, they confided that far from taking away their own happiness, the experience actually gave them joy too.)
- This book. It was my ringside view of this experiment that helped convince me I had to write about generosity.

So in the end their gift is a meaningful demonstration of what can happen when you turbocharge a financial gift with Internet-powered audacity. The beautiful ripple effects are there for all to see.

Few people get the chance to give away $2 million. But it's truly not the amount that matters. Any act of kindness can be amplified. All it may take is a willingness to dream a little and to be brave.

That's because we're in an era like none other in history. New superpowers are at our disposal. It's time to embrace them.

GRATITUDE BREAK

We're about to begin part 2 of our journey, in which we'll roll up our sleeves and consider the practical angles of making generosity infectious. We'll hear dozens of stories of infectious generosity in action and explore the things that we personally could do. But before we go there, let's pause for one moment. There is one more aspect of generosity we need to consider first.

Infectious generosity starts with what's going on inside our own heads. We need to find a pathway to the *generosity mindset* that is at the heart of all giving. Given the daily challenges of life, it's easy to spend much of our time wrapped up in our own concerns. But in that state of mind, it will be nigh impossible to imagine doing anything for anyone else.

So how do you build a generosity mindset?

It may start with being generous to *yourself*. Many of us feel choked by a sense that we're not worthy. In that frame of mind, it's hard to look outward. Dan Harris gave a beautiful (and hilarious) TED Talk on how to nurture compassion for yourself. After a humiliating 360-degree review—in which his family, friends, and colleagues informed him he was self-centered, dramatic, and mean to junior staff—Harris tried everything to fix it. Already a meditator (but, as he realized, "still a schmuck"), he signed up for a nine-day loving-kindness retreat, "which to me sounded like Valentine's Day with a gun to my head." He was unimpressed when the retreat teacher informed him that upon seeing his demons, he was to tell them: "It's okay, sweetie, I'm here for you."

For six days, he told the TED audience, he was held captive by his anger and self-centeredness. Finally, on day six, he caved. He refused to call himself "sweetie," but he nonetheless put his hand on his heart: "I know this sucks but I've got you." And he had an epiphany. "If I wanted to be less of a jerk to other people, I needed to start by being less of a jerk to myself."

Building on that, we should seek to engage the single most important tool for activating our best selves: *gratitude*. As the Mystery Experiment demonstrates so powerfully, when we believe we've been given something, it feels natural and joyful to pass that gift onward. And it's surprising how much we *could* be grateful for.

New TED employees once introduced themselves by sharing some things they were grateful for in their lives. One engineer started out like most others: "My parents, my sister, my friends, my education, nature . . ." Then he paused and continued. "The electric grid. How amazing is it that literally everywhere you go, you can plug in a device and have access to unlimited power?" It was such a great response.

What about my own gratitude list? After my loved ones, it includes: Science. Plumbing. Central heating. Books that shaped me.

The Internet (despite everything). Trees. The night sky. The invention of scuba diving. Humans' astonishing ability to reimagine and reshape the future. The point is that almost every aspect of our modern lives can be framed as something to be grateful for. The vast majority of our ancestors lived under the regular threat of hunger, sickness, danger, discomfort, or violence. Most of you reading this book do not live such a life.

A beautiful way to start each day is to ponder one single thing that you're grateful for. Try and pick something new every day for a month. Then rinse and repeat. From that starting point, it's natural to want to share something good with others.

So to prepare us all for what's to come, consider this reflection from the Austrian American Benedictine monk David Steindl-Rast, who has spent many decades pursuing common ground among people of all belief systems. Filmmaker Louie Schwartzberg has a TED video that pairs these words with stunning footage of our beautiful world. If I'm ever feeling small or turned inward, this is my therapy.

Begin by opening your eyes and be surprised that you have eyes you can open, that incredible array of colors that is constantly offered to us for our pure enjoyment. Look at the sky. We so rarely look at the sky. We so rarely note how different it is from moment to moment, with clouds coming and going. We just think of the weather, and even with the weather, we don't think of all the many nuances of weather. We just think of "good weather" and "bad weather." This day, right now, has unique weather, maybe a kind that will never exactly, in that form, come again. The formation of clouds in the sky will never be the same as it is right now. Open your eyes. Look at that.

Look at the faces of people whom you meet. Each one has an incredible story behind their face, a story that you could never fully fathom, not only their own story, but the story of their ancestors. We all go back so far, and in this present moment, on this day, all the people you meet, all that life from generations and from so many places all over the world flows together and meets you here, like life-giving water, if you only open your heart and drink.

Open your heart to the incredible gifts that civilization gives to us. You flip a switch and there is electric light. You turn on a faucet, and there is warm water and cold water, and drinkable water.

Let the gratefulness overflow into blessing all around you. And then it will really be a good day.

Okay, we're ready. . . .

PART TWO

HOW

Everyone can play a part

6

SIX WAYS TO GIVE THAT
AREN'T ABOUT MONEY

Attention. Bridging. Knowledge. Connection.
Hospitality. Enchantment.

et's start with some very good news. Infectious generosity isn't all about writing checks. Far from it. Many of the most awe-inspiring and effective examples of generosity are gifts of time and energy, talent and love, custom-fitted to a specific need. This type of giving is open to everyone.

These gifts can take many different forms: volunteering, simple acts of kindness, or even just a smile offered to someone whose path crosses yours. They all matter. But in this chapter we're going to focus on six gifts of time and attention that have strong potential to spark ripple effects.

1. Shift Attention

The Zen master Thich Nhat Hanh taught that attention is the most precious gift we can give someone. Certainly, all generosity starts right there—a willingness to stop focusing on ourselves and pay attention to someone else and their needs. From that act of connection, anything can happen.

In 2015, Joshua Coombes was working as a hairdresser at a London salon. One day, while walking back from work, he noticed a familiar homeless person on the sidewalk. Most Londoners walk past the homeless every day, as though they were invisible. Not so Joshua. He approached the man and asked him how he was. Then he had an idea. He had his clippers and scissors with him, so he offered the careworn homeless man a free haircut right there on the street.

"In the hour that followed, he told me his story," Joshua writes in his book *Do Something for Nothing*. "We connected and became close." Touched by his experience, Joshua started heading into the streets of London whenever he could, offering haircuts to homeless people. Eventually he cut back to part-time work in order to spend more time on the streets.

Joshua found his new vocation incredibly rewarding. Having established an immediate sense of trust, he found that the people he was meeting began opening up about their lives. Hearing the remarkable and often harrowing stories of his homeless clients was in itself a reward. He was struck by their resilience and courage, and thankful for the time they spent together. Determined to broadcast their stories and shatter lazy assumptions about homeless people, Joshua took to Instagram. He posted "before-and-after-haircut" pictures of his homeless clients, told their stories (in their own words), and signed off with the hashtag #DoSomethingForNothing. He then started to couch-surf with friends and acquaintances all over the world, giving his time to homeless people across fourteen cities in the Americas, Europe, India, and Australia, and broadcasting their stories via social media. Before long, his Instagram fame resulted in collaborations with brands and NGOs.

Joshua has garnered over 150,000 Instagram followers, who have been moved by the stories he shares. When Joshua posted crowd-funding appeals to fix temporary accommodation for his friends, the cash flowed in. #DoSomethingForNothing became a social movement, with Joshua's inbox full of messages from people pledging their help. Joshua writes that one of the most powerful choices we make each day is to be aware of how we interact with those around us. "Give the benefit of the doubt to other people until they prove us otherwise. . . . How difficult is it to say hello?"

The truth is it *can* be difficult. We spend much of our time lost in our own worlds. We're often reluctant to focus on the issues that others are dealing with. They will only complicate our lives. So we put up shields. And that means that many of the people who could really use our attention never feel seen. The generosity of attention is therefore the generosity of being willing to be a little uncomfortable, to take down those shields, to give up a little time, to risk coming to care about someone else.

This type of generosity is even harder for introverts. I know because I am one. Our internal worlds are our happy place. External human interactions take that extra bit of energy. However, when we do connect, it can feel so special. And deep one-on-one human conversations may be a lot easier than the hell of trying to make small talk at a party. Even if you're an introvert, this type of attention shift may turn out to be rewarding.

One important caveat. In some circumstances it may be dangerous to initiate engagement with a stranger, especially for women. I'm not suggesting you put your personal safety at risk. Be ready to be generous. But also be wise.

What about the critique that Joshua's interventions aren't tackling the underlying systemic problems that cause homelessness? Personally, I'm willing to grant hero status to those who are ready to do their bit to make things better for someone else, even if they're operating in a flawed system.

No one is suggesting that individual acts of kindness should be a substitute for tackling systemic issues. On the contrary, they help prepare the way. If we don't practice generosity with each other, system change has no chance. Every act of generous engagement, no matter how small, can start someone on a journey of immense consequence. Here's another instance of that.

John Sweeney grew up in Ireland. He felt invisible. As a child he was bullied by other children. Even by his teachers. "I felt like the loneliest child in the world; like I had nothing and no one," he told my research assistant Kate. Years later, as an adult, he had a pivotal experience that revealed the value of paying attention. He had seen a homeless young woman on the streets of Cork, so he bought her a hot meal and stopped for a chat. Through poverty and chronic disease, she had struggled to care for her three children. She felt completely invisible.

"I want you to know that I care about you, even though I don't know you," John told her. "You absolutely matter and I see you." The experience brought both of them to tears. "The fact that you stopped means the world to me," the woman told him.

John told the story to his children, who passed the word along. One of the kids' friends—a young boy named Isaac—was soon Christmas shopping in the neighborhood and ran into the same woman. Isaac decided to give her fifty euros—his entire Christmas pocket money—to buy Christmas presents for her three children. The children and their mum had completely given up hope of celebrating Christmas. The story spread and ended up making national news.

Realizing that paying attention to a stranger, even for a moment, was a powerful way of spreading kindness, John found a way to make it easy for others to do just this. He had heard about the Italian tradition of *caffè sospeso*—"suspended coffee." The idea is simple. Customers at a café buy an extra "suspended coffee" on top of their own—a pay-it-forward gift that may be claimed by anyone. This could be a poor or homeless person. Often, however, the claimants are people who are simply having a rough day. A kind gesture from a stranger can be all it takes to show them that they matter and make life bearable—and even beautiful. For the gift giver, all it takes is to remember that there are others out there who would love the luxury you're about to indulge in. And that you can easily give them that gift.

John made it his mission to spread suspended coffee to the whole world. It was an idea whose time had come. Within two years, two thousand cafés in thirty-four countries were actively promoting suspended coffee, and the movement now has five hundred thousand followers on Facebook.

He receives daily messages of appreciation from both café owners and suspended coffee participants. One man wrote to him from Philadelphia: "John, you don't know me, but the impact your message has had on my life has been profound." The man had heard John speak and was inspired to make friends with a homeless drug addict, buying him a coffee every day for two months. During this time he came to care deeply about his new friend. So he paid for two months of accommodation for the man and a course of rehab—on condition that "you work hard and turn your life around." The former drug addict did just that, and enrolled at Philadelphia University, the ripple effect of an act of kindness that started many years earlier and many miles away.

The Generous Coffee Shop in Denver, Colorado, takes this concept a step further. As customers enter the café, they are greeted with a large bulletin board arrayed with hundreds of handwritten credit notes:

- TO: A newly single mom. You got this. FROM: A single mom ($10)
- TO: Someone studying for the bar exam. FROM: Someone doing the same ($5)
- TO: Stranger with a broken heart. FROM: Soren and Ellie ($6)
- TO: Someone struggling in the first year of starting their own business. FROM: Someone who has made it (it gets better!) ($6)

The free coffee and cake are made that much sweeter by being gifted from a stranger: a stranger who is not only generous, but one who empathizes with what you're going through, cares about you, and wants to see you pull through.

You don't have to set up a global organization to exercise this type of generosity. All you have to do is shift your attention to someone else and their story. Whether you stop and have a meaningful connection with a person in need or spend thirty minutes researching a cause you think might matter, you have already begun your generosity journey. You've become willing to give the gift of attention. And if you stay open to continuing the journey, it just may have consequences you could never imagine.

2. Build Bridges

In our connected era, there's a type of generosity that matters more than ever: a willingness to reach out to those with whom we're in conflict. Many disputes today play out in public online. Huge audiences can become glued to online feuds. What if we could bring a satisfying resolution to more of these conflicts?

It's hard to reach out to our critics. This is a particularly challenging form of the generosity mindset. You are sacrificing your personal comfort for the greater good of bringing people together. But if you're successful, there's a powerful knock-on benefit: You are helping change the tone of public discussion today. That's a gift to all of us.

Dylan Marron is used to haters on the Internet. As a proudly progressive content creator, he made a series of social-justice-oriented videos for social media, covering topics like police brutality and transgender people's experience of bathrooms. Marron learned quickly that "the way to skyrocket through the algorithm" was to paint the world in black and white, with a heavy dose of snark and sarcasm. As his views rocketed up, however, so did the aggressive comments from strangers: "You're a piece of shit"; "You are a waste of oxygen"; even death threats.

Reeling from the barrage of hate, Marron developed an unexpected coping mechanism. He messaged a few of his trolls, asking if they would like to get on the phone with him. He wanted to prove to himself that they were human beings.

In his TED Talk, Marron describes his first phone conversation with someone who had trolled him: an eighteen-year-old American called Josh who'd told him he was a moron, and that being gay is a sin. While they were unable to see eye to eye on religion, Dylan and

Josh were able to bond over their experience of being bullied in high school and a mutual love of the movie *Finding Dory*.

"Did our single phone conversation radically heal a politically divided country and cure systemic injustice? No, absolutely not, right?" Dylan said. "But did our conversation humanize us to each other more than profile pictures and posts ever could? Absolutely." Dylan was so moved by his encounter with Josh, he created a podcast series called *Conversations with People Who Hate Me*. As an Internet social justice warrior, Dylan realized he had become trapped in an echo chamber. Maybe, he reflected, "the most subversive thing you could do was to actually speak with the people you disagreed with, and not simply at them"—despite the feeling of intense vulnerability.

As Dylan demonstrated, so often the key to bridging is to have a voice conversation with your foe—or even get face-to-face.

For twenty-two years, Craig Watts was a contract chicken farmer in North Carolina. Each year, he raised seven hundred thousand broiler birds in factory-farm conditions for the food giant Perdue Farms. In 2014, Watts was fed up with what he viewed as Perdue Farms' dishonest marketing and the exploitation of farmers such as himself. He was also uncomfortable with the obvious suffering of the birds. So he took an audacious step. He sought to engage with someone who had every reason to hate him. Leah Garcés was a vegan animal-rights activist. Craig invited her to visit him at his house and film conditions at his farm: an act that put his whole livelihood in danger.

"Before I met Craig, I had not an iota of sympathy for these farmers," Leah later told a podcast called *Changed My Mind*. "He represented everything for me that I had been fighting against, up until that moment that I met him. It was a big shock to my core to find myself sitting in his living room, poring over papers, hearing his story, and being moved by his personal suffering."

The pair made a video together exposing the shocking conditions at Craig's farm. It's believed to be the first time that an industrial-scale chicken farmer had willingly opened his barn doors to a film crew. The video attracted a million views in twenty-four hours and coverage in *The New York Times, The Washington Post, Wired,* and *Vice.* It also sparked a documentary. Leah was left inspired by the experience. "If I put myself in these uncomfortable situations, who else could I be making a partnership with?" she thought.

This led to her sitting at the table with Jim Perdue himself, the CEO of Perdue Farms and the villain of her documentary. She was determined to find common ground. And she did. A couple of years later, Perdue came out with its first animal welfare policy. Although she had been criticized on social media for meeting with Perdue, the results speak for themselves. Leah now leads Mercy for Animals, one of the world's most effective organizations pressing for the reform of factory farming.

Our current moment needs this type of bridging more than ever. Our political and cultural differences have been alarmingly amplified in recent years, to the point where many people live in an echo chamber that promotes disgust at the other side. Indeed, the loudest voices on social media don't *want* anyone on the other side to be shown respect.

That makes it extraordinarily hard to reach out a hand of friendship. Which is why doing so may take a courageous act of generosity—generosity to the person on the other side of the issue, and generosity to the public commons, which is in urgent need of dialogue. To quote the website of the organization BridgeUSA, "Let's f*cking talk to each other." The very act of bridging can create inspiring and surprising ripple effects.

Ciaran O'Connor grew up in Manhattan. Both his parents were liberal journalists, with his dad fond of recounting how he was once tear-gassed for protesting the policies of President Richard Nixon. Growing up in New York City, Ciaran always thought of himself as somebody who valued diversity, with friends of all different races and from all socioeconomic strata. Embracing liberal values, he became a campaign staffer for Barack Obama and later for Hillary Clinton. When he started working for the US-based bipartisan bridging organization Braver Angels, however, he found himself becoming friends with someone he never would have expected . . . a Republican.

That Republican, John Wood, Jr., was also a liberal as a young man in Culver City, California. But then his life changed. Marrying a soldier, moving to a military town, experiencing a religious conversion, and reading Ayn Rand's novel *Atlas Shrugged* fundamentally changed his mindset, and he became vice chairman of the Republican Party of Los Angeles County. However, like Ciaran, he became convinced that seeking common ground was essential for his country's future. So he, too, joined Braver Angels.

"Even if people don't agree, we can see ourselves in each other's stories," Ciaran told Kate. "Stories which are unique to each person but where common emotions and values get surfaced." For Ciaran, John is "kind and smart. Confident yet humble." For John, Ciaran "cares about people, regardless of their politics. Everything he does he does to make this country a better place for everyone." The two now tour colleges and campuses together, speaking about how their friendship bridges political differences and singing duets from the musical *Hamilton*.

I'm not saying that you should always assume good intentions. In some cases, we may have real cause to be wary. But what we can't do is to assume bad intentions. Instead, first seek to listen and to understand. There was a line my mother must have spoken a thousand times, one I wish was wired into all social media platforms: "Don't judge until you know their story."

That's the key to bridging. Think of everyone as a fellow human being with a unique story. Be ready to truly listen to those we instinctively disagree with.

That needn't mean that everything has to end up as a frustrating compromise. Braver Angels makes clear that the organization's goal is not to settle for a "mushy middle." Their manifesto urges people to embrace both of the following: "We state our views freely, fully, and without fear" and "We treat people who disagree with us with honesty and respect."

That basic respect can change everything.

An initiative in Taiwan shows one way that bridging can be done on a serious scale. Taiwan's inaugural minister of digital affairs, Audrey Tang, has helped launch a program called vTaiwan, which brings citizens together online with the goal of discovering areas of agreement rather than disagreement. Based on a platform called Polis, which draws maps of how people's views relate to each other, vTaiwan has been used to discover bridging on multiple issues. For example, during an intense debate on whether Uber should be regulated or not, vTaiwan discovered that what united everyone was a desire for safety. That discovery pointed to a clear direction for simplified regulation that both sides were happy with.

Everyone on the Internet can play an important bridging role. Even an act as simple as a kind reply to a nasty online comment can influence how someone else decides to respond. Your single bridging comment may not immediately go viral, lead to a podcast, or get mentioned in *The New York Times*. But acting in a way that could inspire even one other person to bridge could create waves you'd never imagined. I believe this form of generosity will be key to our building the public commons the world needs.

3. Share Knowledge

As the clichéd saying goes, teach someone to fish, and you feed them for a lifetime. The knowledge acquired by humans over the centuries has value without limit. The fact that it can be freely transferred from one mind to another is one of our species' superpowers. In countless circumstances, the single greatest gift we can give is knowledge— knowledge to solve a problem, fill a need, or open a pathway forward.

Teachers have devoted their lives to this form of infectious generosity. But we're in an era when anyone can be a teacher in one form or another. YouTube and TikTok have created vast new platforms for the amplification of knowledge transfer.

Back in 2004, a hedge fund analyst named Sal Khan began offering math lessons to his cousin, Nadia, who was struggling with unit conversion. As Nadia improved in math class, word got around and Sal was deluged with tutoring requests from other members of his extended family. Within a couple of years, scheduling became a real issue, but happily a new tool called YouTube had recently launched. Sal began recording his lessons and posting them there so that his relatives could watch at their own convenience. He discovered something surprising. His family actually *preferred* the video lessons. It meant they could learn at their own pace, replaying as needed. And the videos were always there to refer back to. More and more people started watching, and before long Sal chucked in his job to focus on building out Khan Academy, which offers free online education to anyone in the world. Since then, their lessons have been viewed more than two *billion* times. And the story doesn't stop there. In 2023, Khan Academy became an early adopter of AI. Sal foresees a future in which children can have their own AI-powered tutor able to offer personalized guidance on every aspect of learning.

When you think of the sharing of knowledge as an example of generosity, it can make that sharing even more powerful. Our single biggest piece of advice to someone coming to speak on the TED stage is to think of the talk not as an opportunity to pitch something (a business or a cause) but rather as a *gift*. It is a chance to freely share valuable ideas with the audience. Those ideas have the potential to impact a listener's life for years to come. When speakers focus their talks that way, the audience is much more likely to embrace them and hang on every word.

One of the beautiful things about sharing knowledge is that even after you've given it away, you still own the knowledge for yourself. As Thomas Jefferson put it, "He who lights his candle at mine receives light without darkening me." The giver is certainly giving up the right to exclusive use of that knowledge—plus the time and effort it takes to share it. But the relative benefit to the recipients may massively outweigh those sacrifices. And once knowledge has been received, it can readily be passed on, creating the potential for beautiful chain reactions of unlimited consequence.

If you possess knowledge that others may benefit from, consider how you could share it to create ripple effects. What may take you a few hours to prepare and act on could light up someone's life—and that could just be the beginning. As the civil rights leader Ella Baker said, "Give light and people will find a way."

4. Enable Connections

In our connected age, the networks we have access to matter more than ever. Therefore, one of the most important forms of viral generosity is to help people connect with others.

The simplest way to do this is to make an introduction. It's a type of generosity that is often overlooked. Yet as the psychologist and TED speaker Adam Grant has argued, it can be fairly easy to give, and unbelievably valuable to receive. It may take only a few minutes, but if done thoughtfully, it can change someone's life. Ask many people how they met their partner, got their dream job, or found the perfect collaborator for their creative project, and the answer will often be the same. Someone—a friend, a neighbor, a colleague—introduced them to the right person. What you're effectively doing is giving someone else access to your network of resources. And those introductions can have exponential consequences.

In her TED Talk, Elizabeth Dunn spoke of the joy she and her friends got from welcoming a family of Syrian refugees to Vancouver. There were physical gifts involved to be sure—setting up a home, providing groceries and clothes, for example—but several years later, the refugees insisted that what was just as important was being incorporated into a community and all that that meant for their daily lives. They told Kate it felt like they had become part of a big family.

Waqas Ali and Sidra Qasim grew up in rural Pakistan and dreamed of doing something meaningful in the world. Their village was known for its shoemaking, and they tried to build a business, tapping into the skills of local craftspeople. But it was hard going. A visitor from Germany, Ulrike Reinhard, visited their workspace and performed an act of generosity that proved transformative. She *connected them* to her network of friends and contacts. That act led to an invitation to visit the United States and assistance with the necessary visa.

"Neither Sidra nor I had even sat on a plane at the time. We had no idea how expensive hotels and housing would be," Waqas told me. But another set of connections took care of that. Waqas was granted a fellowship by Acumen, the global nonprofit tackling poverty via entrepreneurship, and its San Francisco network provided them free accommodation and new introductions, including their first investor. "That trip changed our life."

Back in Pakistan, they launched a Kickstarter campaign for their first revolutionary shoe design. They needed a minimum of $15,000 in seed funding. I had an inside view of what happened next. My partner, Jacqueline, the head of Acumen, reached out to her network, which just happened to include marketing guru Seth Godin. He blogged about the campaign. They smashed through their target, raising a total of $100,000, at the time the biggest Kickstarter campaign ever originating from Pakistan.

Since then, Waqas and Sidra have been unstoppable, immigrating to the United States and building a fast-growing Brooklyn-based shoe company, Atoms, which has attracted more than two hundred thousand customers. But even as the orders flew in, they resolved to carry forward the spirit of generosity that had helped them get started, funding a series of projects back in Pakistan. During the pandemic they created and donated four hundred thousand beautifully designed face masks to local communities. Most recently, they launched a program for up-and-coming creatives called Introducing, by which they identify new talent, become their first paying client, give them business coaching, and introduce them to their fast-expanding network of influencers.

"I can't recall a time in our journey when people haven't shown us generosity in one form or another," said Waqas. "So it's the most natural thing in the world for us to pass it on. Sure, it takes some extra effort. But we love doing it."

What's notable about this story is that everyone benefits. Those who helped Waqas and Sidra on their journey were energized and excited by them. Every act of generosity along the way created significant ripple effects that are spreading to this day.

The hardest thing about granting access to people is our fear that somehow we'll annoy our friends by imposing a new responsibility on them. So it's right to be thoughtful in how we make introductions. We shouldn't, for example, simply share email addresses. Instead, take the time to write to people to explain why you want to make an introduction and get their permission to do so. In so many cases, *everyone* in a network benefits when special new people are added to it.

Sometimes it's possible to connect people at a whole new scale. When the Nigerian biology student Ada Nduka Oyom applied to lead the Google Developers Group at the University of Nigeria, she didn't even have a laptop, only a clunky secondhand phone that kept crashing. There were almost no other women in the Developers Group seeking a career in tech.

At a global event for programmers in 2016, Ada was frustrated at the lack of attention given to African women developers. "I felt it was a kind of injustice," she commented, "because there were a lot of women who were doing amazing stuff. . . ." She decided to do something about it, and founded the nonprofit She Code Africa (SCA) in 2016. Her main goal, when she started, was to broadcast "stories of African female software engineers doing awesome things." So she took to Facebook and started interviewing her female developer friends. The stories generated buzz, and Ada expanded to Medium and other channels. Eventually she started to act as a link between her interviewees and people who wanted to work with them, and her org took on additional roles, such as running training camps and other meetups.

As of 2023, there are more than ten thousand She Code Africa members across fifteen African countries, a thriving community in which the power of connection is manifest to all.

The impact on the world of generous connectors can hardly be overstated. In my own life, when I explored a move to the United States in 1993, I met a woman called Sunny Bates at a publishing conference. She connects people like no one else I've ever met. She made it so much easier for me to set up a publishing business here. And it was she, a few years later, who insisted I should come check out the TED conference. If you've ever watched a TED Talk, somewhere in the causal history of that talk is Sunny Bates.

Introduce. Connect. Convene. This is how our social networks are broadened and deepened. And the richer our networks are, the greater chance that infectious ripple effects can take off through shared ideas, resources, and inspiration.

5. Extend Hospitality

As a child, I had the great good fortune of living for a few years in Afghanistan before the country became racked by war. Our family was able to travel to explore the country's breathtaking beauty. But even more memorable than the majestic Bamiyan Valley or the vivid blue lakes of Band-e Amir was the extraordinary hospitality shown to us. Strangers would welcome us into their modest homes to drink sweet tea with them. There was never a request for anything. It was just the building of human connection. And what's remarkable to me is that even though the gift of a cup of tea may seem like a small thing, it's still in my head all these years later. It still informs how I think of Afghanistan. Even after decades of watching news reports of violence, my inner voice insists: "The people of Afghanistan are the world's most generous."

It's not just me. After 9/11, a budding British diplomat, Rory Stewart, spent twenty months walking through Iraq and Afghanistan, staying in the homes of people he met along the way. He wrote that his deepest lesson was the discovery of the kindness of strangers. Indeed, he owed his life to it.

My Afghan experience made me wonder whether hospitality is in part a response to the dangers faced by travelers: the more challenging the landscape, the more hospitable the people. Certainly across the mountains and deserts of the Mideast, hospitality is one of the most deeply held values. It's also a core value of Islam.

But all over the world, people express hospitality in different ways and usually consider it both a duty and a joy. Back in 2016, the Danish concept of hygge (pronounced "hyooga") became a global phenomenon. It stands for a feeling of coziness, comfort, well-being. It finds its best expression when a group of friends or neighbors gather in front of a fire and simply relax in each other's company. Proponents of hygge see it as one of life's deepest, simplest pleasures. And today it's a form of hospitality that all of us—not just the Danes—can know about and enjoy.

In his remarkable book *Human Universals,* anthropologist Donald Brown documents that hospitality is one of hundreds of human behaviors that have been observed in *every single culture* ever studied. But if hospitality is so ubiquitous—and so pleasant—is it really a form of generosity? Well, yes. Quite apart from any costs involved, it takes effort to invite someone over, whether friends or possible future friends. It's easier just to watch the next episode of the TV series you're into. Indeed, I worry that the growing demands on our time and attention are sometimes crowding out our desire to be hospitable. Even a decade ago, Guy Trebay wrote in *The New York Times* that traditional dinner parties were under threat, thanks to crowded schedules and the ubiquity of handheld devices. That's too bad. Hospitality is a key expression of both our generosity and our humanity. Losing it makes life sadder and smaller.

So how can hospitality contribute to *infectious* generosity? You don't need the Internet for this one. Hospitality taps into our deepest instincts for connection to one another. And each experience of it evokes a desire to reciprocate. *Thank you so much for an incredible evening. It's our turn next.*

But there are ways to make our gatherings even more powerful. Often when people gather, conversations revolve around the latest political outrage or simply small talk about our families and homes. That's fine. But things can move to a whole new level if you can at some point shift the conversation away from opinion or banter and toward a deeper connection. Jacqueline and I love hosting dinners that are anchored by a single conversation thread—so-called Jeffersonian Dinners, or Whole Table Dinners.

There are plenty of resources out there—including a short TED Talk by Jeffrey Walker—on how to host these effectively. For us, the key is to encourage people to open up, to move away from opinion and toward feeling. Questions that can engage a dozen people for an entire evening include:

- What have you seen recently that gives you hope?
- What is something you're worried about right now that few other people are worried about? How might we respond to it?

- What is something or someone that you feel gratitude for that we couldn't have guessed?
- What are you dreaming about: for yourself, for your family, for this community, or for the world at large?
- What is something you long to see better supported?

Such an evening can connect people deeply and lead to new relationships and new plans. It's true that you could call a meeting at work and put one of these questions on the agenda. But it feels entirely different when you're gathering in someone's home and sharing a meal. This is tapping into ancient human rituals that bind us together and make us want to be there for one another.

Oh, and such dinners can lead to surprising ripple effects. For example, encouraged by the single-conversation model suggested by Thomas Jefferson, James Madison hosted a series of dinners in 1787 with delegates from different states. They provided many of the key insights—and human connections—that led to the drafting of the United States Constitution.

For more ideas on how to host a memorable gathering capable of causing ripple effects, watch Priya Parker's insightful TED Talk. But know that even if all you do is to invite guests to your home for a cup of tea, your act of generosity may still be inside their heads for years to come.

6. Create Enchantment

And that brings us finally to a form of infectious generosity that is especially potent for artists of any kind—musicians, painters, photographers, entertainers, writers—and indeed for anyone with a creative spirit.

Pioneering artist Lily Yeh had everything going for her. She had a prestigious career as an art professor and exhibited at famous galleries. She also enjoyed family life, raising a young son. But something was missing. "I felt an emptiness inside," she told an audience at TEDxCornellUniversity.

Then Yeh had a life-changing encounter. She was approached by the dancer and choreographer Arthur L. Hall to undertake a community art project in a derelict, abandoned plot in her home city of Philadelphia.

"I was interested but totally scared," Yeh recalled. "I had little resources and no experience in working outdoors in a community setting. I wanted to run away, but I did not want to see a coward in the mirror. So I stepped into the project."

The community project became the Village of Arts and Humanities, an art park full of trees, sculptures, and mosaics created by local adults and children in collaboration with Yeh. "Through working with the children, we gained the trust of the adults. We made many mistakes along the way, but when we got it right, we found our voice. It was authentic and fresh." The art park was so enchanting that busloads of tourists came to visit.

Community art became the focus of Yeh's life. She sought to serve people trapped in conditions of destitution, oppression, and pollution, bringing beauty into their built environments with collaborative works of public art. This led her to a creative partnership with Kenyan gallery directors Elimo and Philda Njau, working in Korogocho, a slum next to a vast rubbish dump on the outskirts of Nairobi. "As our brightly colored images began to emerge, the mood of the community began to change," said Yeh. "When we dared to place freshly carved angels on top of an abandoned quarry to guard and bless this community, the spirit of the people soared." It was a partnership that was to last more than a decade.

Yeh's work led her to a profound realization: that creating beauty in public space is profoundly healing and transformative for communities. Like a campfire, "it brings light, warmth, hope, and it beckons people to join in."

Yeh's entire career is a beautiful example of the infectious generosity of enchantment. People need money, food, shelter, and healthcare, to be sure. But we also yearn for beauty, wonder, laughter, transcendence—all elements of enchantment. Those who can enchant can offer a gift of immense value. Lily Yeh could have gone for traditional artistic recognition and money. Instead, she chose to devote her life to bringing beauty to downtrodden communities. And time and again she has seen what this can do. "It's possible to transform the violent energy of our time into a culture of kindness."

There are delightful instances of this form of generosity all over the world. In 2020, St. Mark Street, Gloucester, England, was a terraced street of gray-painted houses. During the depressing early days of the pandemic, local artist Tash Frootko volunteered her time to propose a dramatic redesign, coordinated along the entire street, with the houses painted in a kaleidoscope of colors: from turquoise to lemon peel to emerald green. The tenants and landlords of St. Mark Street liked the idea, and the street was transformed. Word spread, and Frootko began painting three adjoining streets to create Gloucester's "Rainbow Square."

Other artists have found ways to transform neglected spaces with beautiful creations that have enchanted the people in their community and beyond. In Lyon, France, an artist known as Ememem works with quiet dedication, filling hundreds of potholes, cracks in walls, and other "wounds of the urban fabric" with intricate, glittering mosaics. The results are more alluring to many than the pristine state ever was. Ememem's stated motivation is to "repair the streets and the hearts of those who tread it."

New York–based NGO Sing for Hope has placed hundreds of artist-decorated pianos in parks, on street corners, and in subways in New York and around the world, for anyone to play. Busy New Yorkers may be stopped in their tracks by a crazily colorful, beautiful instrument in the middle of a street. "As soon as someone sits down and plays, everyone stops and gathers around . . . ," commented one passerby. "You have this immediate moment of community."

The pandemic was a hard time for many musicians. Knowing the power of music to enchant and connect, musicians both amateur and professional around the world offered their time and skills to those who were most isolated and lonely. In locked-down Florence, a city devastated by Covid, operatic tenor Maurizio Marchini serenaded the city from his balcony. The performance was viewed 4.5 million times on Twitter. Meanwhile, in Lewisham, England, saxophonist Chloe Edwards-Wood and a musicians collective called Give a Song toured the streets, offering socially distanced performances to vulnerable and self-isolating residents watching from their windows. Covers of Bob Marley's "Three Little Birds" and Martha and the Vandellas' "Dancing in the Street" proved particularly popular, bringing some residents to tears.

Others, while not musicians themselves, enchant the world by spreading the music of others. In South Waziristan, Pakistan, music has always been used to connect and resolve conflict. The traditional *attan* folk dance is based on unity and bringing people together. When the Pakistani Taliban gained control of the area in 2005, however, music making was banned. "But slowly that culture began to fade, and the dhol [drums] fell silent," Waziristani singer Maqsood Rehman told Al Jazeera. Post-2016, with the Taliban ousted, conservative values meant it was still a challenge to perform music and keep the culture alive. Enter twenty-two-year-old mobile phone shop owner Waheed Nadan. He connects Waziristani musicians to their audiences simply by uploading their music to Facebook and YouTube. Some of his YouTube videos have hundreds of thousands of views. "Aman Mobile Zone [Nadan's shop] has done a huge service for musicians from South Waziristan," a Waziristani singer told Al Jazeera. "I would say that we have sung songs for South Waziristan, but he has been the one to take it to the people."

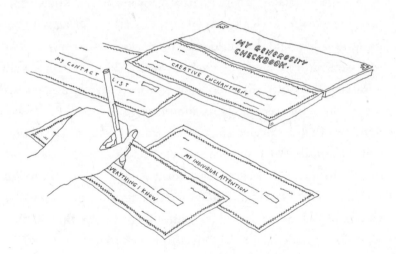

Engage, bridge, teach, connect, host, enchant. As this brief tour shows, each of these nonmonetary forms of giving contains the potential to turn a single act of kindness into a beautiful chain reaction. You may be limited in how much time and energy you can offer. But infectious generosity needs only one moment to ignite. When that moment comes, will you be ready with the match?

CATALYSTS OF CONTAGION

How to shift generosity from invisible to viral

What makes the difference between a generous act that has little impact and one that sends ripples across the world? Everything hangs on this!

To make generosity turn exponential, the first challenge is simply to get it noticed. One of the deep flaws in our psychology is that our attention is biased. It locks onto things that would have once threatened our survival. Threats of all kinds. Suspicious behavior. Anything that might harm us or our families.

Meanwhile, stories of goodness are lovely, but . . . you know . . . they can wait.

I come from the media world and over my whole working life have observed the dilemma that industry faces. Issues that are significant are often complex and daunting. A front-page story about a policy to boost innovation in universities is going to get outsold by a tabloid headline shrieking "The Immigrants Are Coming!"

Social media algorithms operate on the same basic principle pioneered by tabloid owners like the media mogul Rupert Murdoch: Capture people's attention by promoting those who express opinions aggressively and who portray people who don't think like them as a horrifying danger.

Threats, outrage, and disgust are compelling. Earnest goodness, alas, is boring.

What to do?

How about making goodness the very opposite of boring? Let's be generous in a way that gives people goosebumps, in a way that inspires them to share stories and act in kind.

What will it take to do that? There are no hard-and-fast rules here. Any unique, authentic act of human kindness has the potential to capture people's imagination. But how can we best position our generosity to create ripple effects?

Even small changes to our approach may make all the difference. Let's say there's a beautiful act of generosity that some people are inspired to pass along to others. If every ten people who hear about that act pass it on to nine other people on average, then news of it will slowly fizzle away. But if that piece of goodness could become just a bit more infectious, so that those ten people pass it on to eleven others on average, then it goes viral. A butterfly flap of benevolence on one side of the world can then trigger a hurricane of kindness on the other.

Here are five practices that can help your actions make the leap from simple kindness to infectious generosity.

1. Unlock Real Emotion

So much of Internet virality is driven by outrage and fear. But any strong emotion will spread. Why not open the door to amazement, excitement, curiosity, wonder, compassion, inspiration? Many of the most beautiful examples of infectious generosity are acts of human kindness that simply move people deeply.

Jimmy Donaldson—aka MrBeast—has mastered the art. His You-Tube channel, devoted in large part to acts of generosity, has more than 180 million subscribers, making him one of YouTube's biggest influencers. How has he managed it? It took years of practice. As a teenager he and his friends spent hours looking at every aspect of viral videos, including their editing style, the wording of their descriptions, and the visual thumbnails selected. But the biggest insight of all: evoke emotion.

Jimmy used this insight to invent a new formula: extravagant, breathtaking acts of generosity, typically to random strangers. Filmed in real-life situations, MrBeast's subscribers get to watch the dumbstruck amazement on the faces of the people to whom he offers gifts: free cars, free houses, a $100,000 check—even a private island. In one video, "1,000 Blind People See for the First Time," viewers witness the inspiring moments when formerly blind people open their eyes straight after a cataract surgery made possible by MrBeast's largesse. Their wonder and joy at seeing their loved ones for the first time is amazing to behold.

This type of success has, however, attracted criticism. Some viewers watching the gifted cataract surgeries were angered that this was not really addressing the underlying problem of inequitable public health services. MrBeast was even accused of exploiting his subjects' suffering for his own self-promotion.

I do believe a line can be crossed when acts of charity are ill considered. Recently there has been a spate of so-called kindness videos in which someone swoops in to conduct an apparently generous act while the cameras are rolling. For example, in 2022 an Australian woman named Maree was given a bouquet of flowers by a stranger and then filmed as she appeared to tear up, before the stranger left. The video rocketed to more than sixty million views on TikTok. But Maree reported that she felt patronized by the incident. "He interrupted my quiet time, filmed, and uploaded a video without my consent, turning it into something it wasn't, and I feel like he is making quite a lot of money through it," she told a local radio station.

Emotion is powerful, and clearly it can be used in an exploitative way. But in MrBeast's case, I don't believe these criticisms hold, for a few key reasons:

1. All the money he gets from YouTube is recycled into further generous acts. He has pledged to give away all the money he makes.
2. In contrast to the example above, he shows respect to his recipients in his storytelling.
3. The good he has achieved is real. For example, one thousand blind people with restored eyesight is an undeniably good turn of events. Now, it's true that even more could be achieved through real system change. There are organizations out there such as the Aravind Eye Hospital, in India, which has found ways to take cataract surgery to extraordinary scale, offering free treatment for millions of patients in need. But by bringing wide awareness to the fact that a low-cost procedure can change someone's life, MrBeast's video might actually help catalyze that system change. And the fact that an act of generosity could perhaps have been better is not a reason to discount the good it achieved.

4. Most important, it's clear from the response to his channel that MrBeast has inspired literally millions of people to increase the role that generosity plays in their lives. Does he also take steps to entertain and generate emotion and thereby grow his subscriber base? Absolutely. But that's to be admired. He has demonstrated powerfully how generosity can become infectious. And if the next step on his journey is to help channel that generosity to ever more thoughtful ends, so much the better. As he told the Joe Rogan podcast: "I like helping people! It's fun for me! . . . I have this ability to go viral and get views, and I want to figure out how to leverage it—basically, build a charity on the back of it."

There are numerous other instances of emotional content used in a powerful way. The journalist-run Instagram account Good News Movement delights its five million followers with deeply moving acts of human goodness. One photo shows a Syrian girl shielding her brother during the February 2023 Turkey-Syria earthquake. The post directs people to donate to Save the Children Emergency Fund to help child survivors. Within twenty-four hours, it had been liked nearly three hundred thousand times. Other videos showcase everyday heroes and heroines such as the flight attendant who holds a terrified passenger's hand or the little girl determined to help wildlife in her local area. It's beautiful that these small acts of generosity can spread quickly to a global audience. This is how we can change the way we think of our fellow humans.

Of course, generosity can never be *just* about emotion. As we've discussed, that can pull us in the wrong direction. We need to apply the wisdom of reflective thinking to our efforts. But without some kind of emotional firepower, generous acts will never get the attention they deserve.

2. Get Insanely Creative

Familiar acts get lost in the noise. When something is done with imagination and flair, people will notice.

A group of friends in Japan were sick of the litter on the streets of Tokyo. But instead of just going out there and tidying up, they decided to do so in a way that would get noticed. They dressed up as samurai warriors and used their acting skills to pick up the trash with drama and panache, stabbing used bottles with swords and flipping trash into the baskets on their backs. It's easy to understand why the videos of them in action have been seen by millions of people on YouTube and TikTok and have attracted many to come join the group, known as Gomi Hiroi Samurai, replicating their efforts in cities across Japan. The power of creativity was used to turn something as mundane as picking up litter into something cool.

This is a familiar theme for Mundano, a street artist, activist, and TED Fellow based in Brazil. As Mundano spray-painted the streets of São Paulo, his attention was drawn to the "invisible superheroes" he encountered. Scraping a living on the margins of society, catadores (trash collectors) wheel their carroças (carts) through the streets, collecting Brazil's recyclable materials. They are paid only a pittance for the waste, but their efforts are responsible for 90 percent of the recycling that goes on in Brazil.

Mundano felt that the catadores should be honored for the vital service they provide. So he put his artistic skills to use. He started to decorate the carroças of the catadores, painting them with vibrant colors, eye-catching designs, and bold slogans—PROUD TO RECYCLE!, MY CAR DOESN'T POLLUTE! Within a few years, he had painted two hundred carroças in several cities.

Mundano realized he was onto something and decided to push

his project further. He started a crowdfunded campaign called Pimp My Carroça, a movement to celebrate and support the world's twenty million trash collectors. With crowdfunding from more than a thousand donors, and with the help of eight hundred volunteers, Pimp My Carroça was launched in three Brazilian cities. Catadores were offered healthcare services—including massage, dentistry, and hairstyling—and protective equipment. Their carroças were fitted out with horns and mirrors. Finally they were beautifully decorated and spray-painted.

Before long, Pimp My Carroça spread to other countries. "By adding art and humor to the cause, it became more appealing," Mundano told us. "[Catadores] are famous now on the streets, on social media, and mass media. . . . They are able to fight back against prejudice, increase their income and their interaction with society."

Creativity is often simply the ability to remix things in a way that's compelling. It's no surprise that the youngest kids in a family are often the most creative. To get noticed, they have no choice. When it comes to the products we sell, or the entertainment we create, we know that those who are most creative are often the most successful.

Even political leaders can gain huge traction through the use of a little creativity.

In 1995, Antanas Mockus was elected mayor of Bogotá. It was a challenging time. Homicide rates and traffic fatalities were high, water and sanitation services were broken, and corruption was rife.

Mockus could have responded with heavy-handed new laws, backed up by a militarized police. Instead, this artist's son chose a different way. He led Bogotá in an audacious social experiment, with creative stunts to encourage prosocial behavior. To tackle traffic fatalities, Mockus hired a team of four hundred mimes to make fun of traffic violators. Law-abiding taxi drivers were invited to join a special club: the Knights of the Zebra. Stars were painted on the streets to mark the places where pedestrians had been killed. In an effort to decrease homicides, Mockus invited citizens to channel their rage by popping balloons (around fifty thousand joined). To tackle water shortages, he filmed himself taking a short shower. Donning a Superman-style cape, he dubbed himself "Supercitizen."

The stunts were wacky but they worked. During Mockus's leadership, water usage dropped by 40 percent, the homicide rate fell by 70 percent, and traffic fatalities dropped by over 50 percent. Mockus's championing of civic engagement resulted in 63,000 citizens paying a voluntary extra 10 percent in taxes. By acting as a Supercitizen, with a dedication to collective leadership and his "respect for life," Mockus ignited these values in the city. To quote him, "Millions of people contributed to the results that we achieved."

Under Mockus, public policy—a topic that, like generosity, is hard to make interesting—became riveting. His acts were the talk of the town. If we want to make the good unboring, we should be ready to embrace similar levels of imagination.

One especially powerful form of creativity is humor. If you make people laugh, you not only win their attention but you also may well disarm their cynicism. Humor is probably the biggest reason for the viral success of the ALS ice bucket challenge of 2014. The videos that celebrities created showing their support for the campaign were heartwarming, to be sure, but it was the hilarity of seeing them soaked in ice water and then nominating their friends for similar treatment that caused the campaign to spread.*

---

* Could it have done more? Some critics think it was more bark than bite, yet ultimately the ALS bucket challenge raised more than $100 million and massively spread awareness of the plight of ALS sufferers. I'll take that kind of "less than perfect" infectious generosity over a typical Internet meme any day.

The Movember movement has raised even more. Men are encouraged to grow a mustache every November—as wacky and weird as you like—to spark conversations about men's health. The humor and the personal engagement have turned it massively viral, allowing them to raise more than $1 billion over eighteen years for causes such as prostate and testicular cancer.

Humor and creativity are tools everyone can use. An hour of dreaming or brainstorming can transform generosity from a one-off act into something whose creative delight generates exciting ripple effects.

3. Dig Deep for Courage

Fortune favors the brave, and nowhere more than in the world of generosity.

Daryl Davis is an African American musician who grew up puzzled by why there were people in his own country who hated him just because of the color of his skin. One day he decided to find out for himself. He reached out to a man called Roger Kelly, who ran the statewide branch of the Ku Klux Klan for the state of Maryland. He invited Kelly to meet in a motel room. Davis went there with his secretary, and Kelly showed up with his bodyguard. Kelly didn't know the musician he was meeting was black.

Needless to say, it was an incredibly tense meeting. At one point everyone leaped to their feet, convinced that a gun had just been loaded. But it was just the sound of ice clunking in a cooler. Even though Davis was horrified at Kelly's conviction that races should be kept separate, somehow the two agreed on another meeting, this time at Davis's home. They continued to meet. Davis even agreed to attend a Ku Klux Klan rally.

CNN heard about this strange relationship and produced a story on it that was seen around the world. What drew them to it? It was Davis's deep courage in being willing to do what almost no one else in his shoes would dare. That courage eventually led to Kelly leaving the KKK. Davis had become a friend. How could he stay? And it led to literally millions of people being inspired by Davis's example of reaching out across a seemingly unbridgeable divide. His efforts have been nationally recognized. As he said in a TEDx Talk (which has itself notched up more than twelve million views), "Ignorance breeds fear. We fear those things we do not understand. If we do not keep that fear in check, that fear, in turn, will breed hatred because we hate those things that frighten us. If we do not keep that hatred in check, that hatred, in turn, will breed destruction."

This is an example of the bridging that we spoke of in the previous chapter. The evident courage at its heart enabled it to inspire millions.

Courage comes in many forms. It sometimes burns bright, as when a Malian man climbed four stories of a building in Paris to save a stranger's toddler dangling from a balcony, lighting up social media with dramatic video. And it sometimes has a longer, slower burn, as when a schoolteacher from Grimsby, UK, walked nine hundred miles during the first Covid lockdown, delivering fifteen thousand meals to his vulnerable students.

To my way of thinking, any sustained challenging act requires a form of courageous generosity. When Covid hit the UK, Captain Tom Moore was ninety-nine years old and very frail, able to get around only with a walker. He wanted to do something to help the National Health Service but couldn't personally give much money. However, he could offer his time and energy. So he announced a unique fundraiser, committing to walk one hundred laps of his garden before his hundredth birthday, an effort sure to take him many days of intense effort. This took genuine courage on his behalf. He wasn't certain he could complete the task. And no one wants to look foolish.

His local newspaper ran a story about his plan and it soon went viral on social media. People were deeply moved by the spectacle of this war veteran slowly, determinedly walking up and down his garden to help the beleaguered doctors and nurses of the NHS. His catchphrase, "Tomorrow will be a good day," became a meme, and he was invited to record a cover of the classic anthem "You'll Never Walk Alone." On his triumphant one hundredth birthday, not only had he completed the walk, he received 160,000 greeting cards and was the oldest person ever to have a number one hit single. A knighthood followed soon after.

His goal had been to raise £1,000. But when someone's generosity turns infectious, all bets are off. The total amount raised mushroomed to £32 *million*.

Captain Moore ended up being killed by the disease he had raised money for. But his final chapter undoubtedly helped save the lives of many others. And his courageous determination inspired hope in millions during the darkest days of the pandemic.

Every act of generosity is meaningful. But those that are carried out with courage may have dramatically greater impact. Courage is not the same as fearlessness. In fact, without fear, there can be no courage. Courage means overcoming your fear. And if you can do that, you may be able to create ripple effects that change the world.

So what happens when you combine creativity and courage? There's a powerful word for it: *audacity*. Audacious dreams attract generosity and audacious acts of generosity can become contagious. We'll dig much deeper into this notion in chapter 12.

4. Reach Out and Collaborate

Collaboration is hard. But when someone figures out how to do it, it becomes a massive amplifier of human intent. One plus one plus one can add up to millions.

As in other cities around the world, when Los Angeles locked down in the early days of the Covid-19 pandemic, a beautiful new ritual came into being. Every evening, at eight o'clock, people would step out on their porches or lean out of their windows, hollering and beating pans to show appreciation for frontline healthcare workers.

The Grammy-winning LA-based rock band OK Go were inspired by the spectacle. With each band member performing remotely, they produced a new music video called "All Together Now." All profits from the song were donated to Partners In Health, a global healthcare charity. "The idea that some good may come from this time of overwhelming tragedy is a light in the dark right now," said lead vocalist Damian Kulash. "As we wrestle with anxiety, every drop of hope is precious. We want to nurture it and share it."

The song lyrics are an anthem to the possibility of global connectedness.

Everything's untouched
But forever changed . . .

Everywhere on earth
Every single soul
Everyone there is
All together now

Deeply moved by the song, a high school teacher got in touch with Kulash. Could she have the sheet music to arrange for her school choir, so that they could also perform it in quarantine? Her request sparked a big idea. They decided to offer their music free to the world, with the aim of uniting a global community of musicians in mass-participation videos. In partnership with the University of St. Thomas Playful Learning Lab, arrangements of the song were made for string orchestra, choir, wind band, and various other types of ensembles. Artists and animators produced animation frames for anyone to color in. Then the call was opened up to artists, students, and schoolchildren who wanted to create art to be featured in the videos.

The response stunned them. They received fifteen *thousand* submissions. To combine them took an intense effort of editing, animating, and mixing, but the result was a series of six inspiring music videos: the #ArtTogetherNow series.

As Kulash said, "It became their version, not ours."

When you look at this project, there's generosity at every single stage: OK Go's willingness to give away their music and spend huge amounts of time in planning and organization. The efforts by several partners to facilitate the project. And the gifts of time and creativity behind every one of the fifteen thousand submissions.

And of course none of it would have been possible without the Internet. When it's at its best, the web can truly inspire. I remember tearing up when I saw Eric Whitacre's first Virtual Choir video, featuring 185 singers from twelve countries. *This is what the Internet was built for.*

The web has enabled collaborations in many unexpected places. K-pop boy band BTS started their career in a garage in 2010.

Their rise was meteoric. By 2020 they had become the world's top-selling artists and won the IFPI Global Recording Artist of the Year Award two years running. They are also the first South Korean band to reach number one on the Billboard Hot 100. Their global following is astronomical, with an estimated *one hundred million fans* across the world on social media.

There's something else remarkable about this fan base (known as ARMY). The largely Gen Z ARMY is expert at hacking social media algorithms to boost BTS hashtags and videos. And they don't stop there. Empowered by their numbers and famously scrappy, they use social media firepower to make the world a better place, both online and offline.

Part of BTS's appeal is indeed the band's firm commitment to alleviating suffering. They sing about youth mental health and well-being, and famously partnered with UNICEF to combat violence against young people. BTS have a dynamic, symbiotic relationship with their fans, each one inspiring the other. When BTS donated $1 million to Black Lives Matter, ARMY matched it in a little over twenty-four hours using the hashtag #MatchAMillion. When BTS and UNICEF launched the hashtag #LoveYourselfBTS to spread messages of hope and self-care to vulnerable young people, it was retweeted eleven million times by ARMY members. These fans also take their activism offline. To celebrate the birthdays of Jungkook and RM, two BTS members known for their environmentalism, members of ARMY coordinated tree-planting efforts worldwide. Thousands of native trees were planted in the Philippines, South Korea, and Brazil, with the new forests named after the band members.

The Internet allows collaborations that were never possible before. Big open-source software initiatives were one of the first striking manifestations of this. Jimmy Wales did the same with information, ushering in the incredible success of Wikipedia, where thousands of volunteers spend countless hours editing millions of encyclopedia entries. I asked Jimmy if it was correct to think of Wikipedia as an example of infectious generosity. "Definitely! If you just spent four hours improving some obscure article in Wikipedia, it isn't uncommon to think about some curious reader, perhaps months or years in the future, who will stumble across your lovely little gift to the world and perhaps have a smile and a wonder at who bothered to do this delightful little thing. Plus . . . it's fun! You get to meet other clever, interesting people and work together on topics that you're interested in."

You can find that spirit all over the Internet. The International Network of Crisis Mappers is a volunteer community of 9,600 experts in more than 160 countries who collaborate and share data. The aim is to predict disasters, crowdsource relevant data, and protect civilians. The network includes policymakers, technologists, researchers, journalists, and hackers. With each one being willing to contribute a little time, they have created a resource of incalculable value. And the efforts of each individual in that community in turn inspire the next individual to join and contribute.

Each time you think about an act of generosity, it's worth asking how you could recruit others to join in. Every crowdfunding campaign is an example of this, as are the numerous giving circles that have cropped up in recent years, often emerging naturally out of Facebook groups or YouTube channels.

Collaboration is not always easy, and occasionally it can backfire. If you run an organization that you've carefully built over many years, it can be hard to build easy collaboration with another org. Who has responsibility for what? If there isn't clarity on roles, things can quickly get chaotic and counterproductive. The key is for everyone to be clear from the outset on how to best divide and conquer.

But if you can find a smart way to spark collaboration, your impact might just rocket. It is likely a much more productive use of your time than simply going it alone and getting lost in the noise. It's also more fulfilling to work this way. When things are hard, you have others to share the load. When things are great, you have others to celebrate with.

So why not ponder how to embark on your infectious generosity collaboration? It could start by hosting a single-conversation dinner party, as discussed in the previous chapter. This time your focus can be on hearing from each other about the issues in your neighborhood—or in the world—that your guests most care about and why. Then ask everyone which of the issues they've heard about that they could imagine getting interested in as a group. There's a good chance that at least one issue will capture the imagination of those gathered. Spend the rest of the time brainstorming whether there's anything you could do together to support that issue. It could be: deciding as a group to volunteer for an afternoon at a local nonprofit. Or planning to research an issue in greater depth, with each person taking on a particular area. Or everyone chipping in a small sum to create a shared donation. Or agreeing to go online to support one another in spreading a meme or a story that is positive for the world. Or teaming up to help a local family in need.

It's possible you'll end up with an idea that makes a real difference *and* that draws you all closer. There's nothing like a common cause to deepen friendship. Local generosity collaborations could be the new book clubs!

You could even go a step further and turn your efforts into a giving circle that can grow over time and attract others. There's a beautiful TED Talk by Sara Lomelin that describes giving circles in action and offers core tips on how to make one work. And she ends with this challenge: "What if every town, every issue, every community had a giving circle with passionate philanthropists like you? In a world that feels heavy, doing philanthropy together fills me with so much joy and hope for the future."

5. Build an Amplifier

As we've seen, striking stories of impact happen when people use the tools of our connected age to amplify their initial efforts. John Sweeney went from a single gift of a coffee to a global movement paying forward gifts of coffee. Sal Khan went from gifting individual videos to setting up an organization devoted to sharing education. Ada Nduka Oyom didn't just connect African women in technology; she built a platform that would allow this to happen at scale.

If you can create such an amplifier, you will take your impact to a whole new level. Obvious examples include:

- A social media group focused on a specific way of helping others.
- A website that connects people concerned about an issue.
- An app that makes it easy to offer advice or summon help.
- A crowdfunding campaign.
- An organization that seeks to advance a cause you care about.

Such efforts may be beyond the resources of most people. We're not all engineers, organizers, or entrepreneurs. But there's no harm in being open to such possibilities. You can start at the level of your neighborhood and see how far you can go. The tools to build movements are getting better all the time. And AI is offering spectacular new possibilities to curate and generate knowledge and creativity. Sometimes all it takes is to be in the right place at the right time, and to find a couple of like-minded souls who would like to help.

At our website infectiousgenerosity.org, we are compiling resources for anyone interested in dreaming about these possibilities.

All Together Now

Emotion, creativity, courage, collaboration, and amplification are each powerful in their own right. In combination, they're electrifying. They can provide the fuel needed for acts of kindness to be noticed and to spread waves of inspiration around the world.

The story of Amy Wolff showcases every single one of these

practices—and demonstrates how a single person, without any expert or insider knowledge, can spark a powerful campaign of infectious generosity. In the spring of 2017, Wolff, a public-speaking coach, heard about the suicide rates of young people in her town of Newberg, Oregon. The statistics were staggering, and she felt shocked and hopeless. She wasn't a therapist. What the heck could she do in the face of this suffering?

She later told the *Sounds Good* podcast that, despite feeling so unqualified, she felt "stubbornly determined to do something, and not be apathetic and wait for someone else."

Years previously, Wolff had had a crazy dream. "I had visions of these yard signs that said 'Don't Give Up,'" she related. "Cheering someone on going through a divorce or kicking an addiction . . . How would I feel if I was in the midst of chaos or trauma or heartache, on my way to work, and in the middle of nowhere I see this *sign* that cheers me on?!"

The Newberg suicide statistics were the catalyst she needed to act on her crazy dream. She ordered twenty yard signs, with Brené Brown–inspired messages of love, hope, and courage: YOU GOT THIS, YOU ARE WORTHY OF LOVE. She got in the car with her husband, kids, and twenty yard signs, on a mission to ask residents of Newberg to stick them in their yards. "This is the dumbest, dumbest idea," Wolff thought as they drove off.

She was wrong. All the strangers they approached in Newberg wanted the yard signs. Local social media channels blew up within hours, with new people wanting signs in their yards, too. Wolff outed herself as the sign maker, started a website, and took new sign orders. It quickly became a global movement, with sign orders coming from every state and from twenty-four countries around the world. And it continues to this day.

Messages have poured into her inbox about the positive impact the signs have had. One man was actually driving toward a site where he planned to commit suicide when he saw a sign reading DON'T GIVE UP. He drove home and opened up to his family about his depression. A shame-ridden drug addict saw this "bright, white thing" as he was driving: a yard sign reading YOUR MISTAKES DON'T DEFINE YOU. He booked himself into rehab.

Wolff didn't make a cent of profit from the initiative. The signs were no-strings kindness: "birthed out of a rallying cry for anyone, anywhere." It seems that this no-strings kindness met a deep, universal need, both for the receiver and the giver.

Starting the program took emotional intelligence, courage, creativity, collaboration, and a determined effort to further amplify the impact. And from that catalytic energy grew a truly beautiful global movement.

There's another crucial catalyst that every single person reading this book can engage in. It deserves its own chapter.

PASS IT ON!

How infectious generosity depends on the stories we tell . . .

n the previous chapter, I offered an array of stories of how people have sparked moments and movements of infectious generosity. But I know you may have lingering doubts. What we see and hear every day can reinforce our skepticism that things are headed in the right direction. Right now the world portrayed in both mainstream media and social media is often a dark one. Everything seems threatening. Politics, technology, crime, culture, and, above all, the scary, dangerous future. Of course, if the world actually is miserable and cruel, then perhaps it's better to know the truth and live with it. But is the world really this way? Many of those who have looked at the actual data believe it isn't.

Steven Pinker's 2018 masterwork, *Enlightenment Now*, painstakingly documents the progress humanity has made globally on pretty much every aspect of life one can measure, including fewer wars, less crime, less poverty, massive social progress, longer lives. In early

2023, I asked him if he felt recent developments had undercut his argument. He did not.

"Human progress is not an argument but a fact," he wrote to me. "That continues to be true, even though the recent terrible setbacks of Covid-19 and Putin's war have undone some of our recent gains. The setbacks are probably temporary, and even they have taken place against a scorecard of continuing progress in the last few years: dozens of countries that have eradicated or reduced a disease; abolished capital punishment, child marriage, or the criminalization of homosexuality; protected or restored ecologically sensitive areas; reduced air and water pollution; safeguarded the rights of women and transgender people; expanded access to electricity, clean water, and schools; and accelerated a transition away from fossil fuels. And the setbacks remind us of what progress actually is: not a miraculous force that makes life better for everyone everywhere all the time but the dividends of human ingenuity, effort, compassion, and good ideas. Wherever these drivers of improvement are weakened, progress will halt or reverse—making it all the more imperative for us to understand, cherish, and enhance them."

I'm on board with Pinker, even if the stories we hear would lead us to believe otherwise. Let's take a moment to consider why today's media landscape is dominated by doom and gloom.

The Unfortunate Logic Behind Media Storytelling

Back when I was a journalist, I once had a job that entailed crafting a world news summary based on the news feeds of the major news agencies. Stories were marked with labels according to how big an item of news the agencies estimated them to be. For example, the

Associated Press reserved the label "BULLETIN" for the items it thought were absolutely giant stories, the biggest of the day.

The philosopher in me started to wonder how it had come to that conclusion. How could you compare the significance of a political drama in one country with the act of a celebrity somewhere else? So I kept track of these stories and pretty soon a pattern emerged.

Very roughly speaking, what it usually took to claim the world's top story would be for one hundred people or more to die in a dramatic or violent way—a bomb blast, say, or a plane crash. There were some subtleties. If children were involved, the number of deaths could be a lot lower. A natural disaster such as a flood in a country that somehow seemed far away would need a lot *more* people to die for it to warrant global interest. But as a rule of thumb, one hundred violent deaths guaranteed you the world's top story.

At first glance, you may find that reasonable. After all, it *is* shocking when a plane goes down and one hundred or more people die. The scenes of grieving families grab our hearts. A story like that can consume the news for days.

But the broader context is left out. In fact I'm guessing you may not know what I'm about to tell you. When you take all causes into account, *more than 170,000 people die every single day*. The plane crash counts for one-seventeenth of one percent of that. Perhaps you'll tell me that deaths from bad health or natural causes aren't so interesting. Maybe. But for almost every single one of those 170,000 deaths, somewhere a family grieved. If you're a mother, would it hurt you more to lose a child in a plane crash or from a common disease? It's about the same, don't you think?

The real headlines should be about the amazing efforts out there seeking to reduce that human suffering. To take just one example: In 1990, despite decades of development aid and medical progress, more than 35,000 children died *every day*. Now, thanks to the heroic efforts of those who have devoted their lives to tackling malnutrition and preventable childhood diseases, that number is less than 14,000.

So I ask you, which is the more significant fact to know about the world? That 100 people died in a plane crash yesterday? Or that 21,000 children who would have died yesterday if the world operated how it did just a few years ago are actually alive?

It is a shocking indictment of mainstream media that few people are ever even given the data to decide for themselves.

There's no evil intent here. Quite the opposite. The world's news editors pride themselves on being able to sift signal from noise in a way that's interesting. They have incredible instincts for what will capture people's imaginations. But they are influenced by two powerful distorting factors:

1. Cognitive Bias: Bad Is Stronger Than Good

All humans are wired to pay more attention to danger than to opportunity. We are complex, improbable beings. It is much easier to hurt us badly than to make us dramatically better. Humpty-Dumpty sitting on his wall might have a thousand opportunities to improve his view somewhat. But he'd be wiser to pay attention to the risk of a single tumble.

This trigger alert for danger has therefore become a foundational part of our psychology, even in a world where many of the dangers that once threatened us have vanished.

A classic social psychology paper from 2001 by Roy Baumeister and others was starkly titled "Bad Is Stronger Than Good." It showed that in many areas of psychology, the dark things in life impact us more strongly, and for longer, than the good things. Good parenting is often forgotten, childhood trauma can last a lifetime. Gains are liked but losses really chew us up. (This is why loss aversion is such a powerful force getting in the way of our generosity.) And definitely when it comes to capturing our attention, the scary, dangerous, and unpleasant will usually trump the noble, hopeful, and kind. As psychologist Rick Hanson puts it: "The brain is like Velcro for negative experiences and Teflon for positive ones." This is a deeply annoying fact about us. But once you know it, you can start to shake it off.

2. Time Bias: Good Happens Slowly, Bad Happens Quickly

The complexity of our human nature applies to the world at large, too, and it leads to another strange asymmetry between good and bad. The universe's natural state is chaos. It takes time to make anything good happen. Typically good things are built piece by piece by large numbers of people. An inventor gets excited by an idea to solve a major problem. She teams up with an entrepreneur. They raise funding from visionary investors and recruit a team to work with them. Ten years later, millions of people's lives are better off. But there is no single moment in that process when a news editor is going to say, "Hold the front page!"

Take cellphones. They've utterly changed the world, benefiting (and sometimes harming) the lives of billions of people. But when, on April 4, 1973, *The New York Times* announced the unveiling of the world's first "wireless" phone, it was buried at the bottom of page 57.

Or take another world changer, penicillin. It was discovered by Alexander Fleming in 1928. Its first mention in *The New York Times* was not until a full twelve years later, buried once again on page 57, despite the promise of its tiny headline: "New Non-Toxic Drug Said to Be the Most Powerful Germ Killer Ever Discovered." Yes, the Second World War was raging at the time, so you can understand the editors' attention being elsewhere. Yet penicillin would play a meaningful role in helping win that war and would one day be estimated to have saved more than 100 million lives, double the number the war took. But to get there, it had to be developed, tested, put into trials, and eventually made standard practice in the world's health systems. Boring. But world changing.

Bad things, on the other hand, can happen in an instant, and be recognized in an instant. A building that took a decade to plan and build can be blown up in a split second. A politician with a lifetime of leadership experience can be ruined by a single ill-advised act. A plane containing two thousand person-years of accumulated life experience can be taken out by a lightning strike.

Therefore . . . Media Distortion

Put those two things together, and we have a big problem. News outlets are mostly focused on answering the question "What's the most dramatic thing that's happened in the last few hours?" Both biases above push them toward stories that make the world seem alarming.

Social media have dialed this up to a further extreme, and for the same reasons. The posts that grab attention and the accounts that attract followers are often those that do the most effective job of being provocative and critical. But the net result is to give us all the impression of a world that's relentlessly hostile, with the hostility coming from groups we perceive as implacably opposed to us.

Of course there are plenty of bad news stories that we really do

need to hear: injustices, abuses of power, genuine threats to our future, among others. But our news systems are hugely amplifying bad news stories of all kinds, and often failing to offset them with reminders of what's going right.

This is troubling. Because our very characters are shaped by the stories we tell ourselves. What we hear shapes what we believe. And what we believe shapes who we are.

So effectively, we're duping ourselves into thinking the world is worse than it is, and that very belief makes us less trusting, less hopeful, and less ready to believe that we can do something about this. Without anyone meaning to, we're talking ourselves into unbridgeable division, mistrust, and dysfunction.

We simply *have* to right this. Some impressive efforts are already under way.

Giving Better Stories Their Rightful Place

A growing number of online sources are committed to a different narrative, anchored in data and a longer-term perspective. They show a world where, yes, there are severe challenges, but where enormous progress is being made.

Check out Future Crunch ("If we want to change the story of the human race in the 21st century, we have to change the stories we tell ourselves") and the Progress Network ("Let's create the future of our dreams, not our fears"). The Good News Network combines heartwarming personal stories with deeper reports of scientific and environmental progress. The Solutions Journalism Network is drawing attention to those who are out there trying to solve problems. David Byrne of the band Talking Heads founded the inspiring site Reasons to Be Cheerful—check out the We Are Not Divided series of articles. Upworthy offers "the best of humanity every day." And there are many other fledgling media efforts looking to share the day's slower, more significant, more hopeful news.

What Mainstream Media Can Do

Once this book is published, I plan to mail a copy to the editors of one hundred of the most influential news organizations and urge them to read this chapter and post a public response. I suspect that many would say that they have, at times, worried about these exact issues, but ultimately it's the dramatic news that sells. If they lose that, they will die. However, there are dozens of smaller steps they could take that would help. And I think they would make their publications and programs *more* interesting, not less:

- Feature every day a data-based story that shows long-term trends of an issue that's important to people *even if the news is good,* i.e., commit to publishing before you know the results of the data.
- Double down on efforts to find stories that show promising inventions, innovations, or ideas.
- In every bad news story, add data that give it context. A plane crashed. But what is the total of deaths from air accidents this year compared with those in prior years? A child has gone missing. But what percentage of children who go missing are eventually found safe? And is the trend getting better or worse?
- Add a regular slot featuring invisible heroes who have done something good for their community.
- Add a regular op-ed titled "My Moonshot Idea . . ."
- Add a regular slot in which your readers are invited to share simple tales of human kindness.
- Add a daily feature titled "Slow News" devoted to significant events of the past *decade* whose importance has only recently become clear.
- Invite the Solutions Journalism Network to offer you a daily story.
- Consider redefining your mission as: "News that matters."

The Stories We Must Tell

If you read that list and found yourself thinking, *Never going to happen, they'll never fix it,* perhaps *you* can help! This is an effort we can all take part in. We are all publishers. Every day, millions of beautiful acts of generosity take place on planet Earth. And almost every single one happens invisibly. If we could notice these acts and share stories about them, it could transform how we think of ourselves and of our fellow citizens.

Now, there's a paradox here. Generous souls often don't want to blow their trumpet. We're taught that acts of generosity should be done with modesty and out of the limelight. Indeed, we often censure those who seem to be flaunting their kindness. But there's a tragic consequence to this: Stories that could cause amplification of generosity are left untold. Which hands over the public conversation space to our darker natures.

How about we fight back a bit? We should set out to discover and share people's generosity, creativity, audacity, and collaboration whenever we can find them. And that includes stories that we know better than anyone else—our own! Far from modestly hiding them, in today's turbulent attention war, we indeed have a moral responsibility to share those stories, too.

I think there's a way to do this that doesn't come across as boasting. I certainly hope so, because I've already shared with you several of mine. Here's what I passionately believe: Every single generous thing I've ever done has been a result of the good fortune I've had at almost every stage of my life. So there's nothing to boast about. I'm simply passing them on, hopeful that they can encourage others. In a similar spirit, I urge you to be willing to share things you do that have brought you and others joy. It's all part of changing the narrative.

MacKenzie's Magic

MacKenzie Scott is doing this. Her divorce from Amazon founder Jeff Bezos in 2019 left her with a fortune valued at as much as $60 billion. She quickly committed "to give the majority of my wealth back to the society that helped generate it, to do it thoughtfully, to get started soon, and to keep at it until the safe is empty." Since then, each year she has made surprise gifts to scores of organizations, totaling multiple billions of dollars. And she has been unafraid of making these gifts public if the organizations so wish. Her announcements are the opposite of self-aggrandizing. Instead, her intention is to celebrate the people she regards as heroes: the people doing the hard work of change. Observers of philanthropy have been stunned by her boldness and her willingness to trust social entrepreneurs with her money without torturing them with endless due-diligence requests or requirements for how the money is spent. If you want to see what it looks like to give publicly without boasting, spend some time on MacKenzie's website yieldgiving.com. It includes some of the most thoughtful essays you'll ever read about philanthropy. Here's a beautiful passage in which she speaks of those who have inspired her own generosity:

> It was the local dentist who offered me free dental work when he saw me securing a broken tooth with denture glue in college. It was the college roommate who found me crying, and acted on her urge to loan me a thousand dollars to keep me from having to drop out sophomore year. And after she saw the difference she made in my life, what was she inspired to do, twenty years later? Start a company that offers loans to low-income students without a co-signer. And how quickly did I jump at the opportunity to support her dream of supporting students like she once supported me? And to whom will each of the thousands of students thriving on those gratitude-powered student loans go on to give? None of us

has any idea. Each unique expression of generosity will have value far beyond what we can imagine or live to see.

It is never just a gift. Gifts carry with them the potential to replicate. And that may happen only if the world comes to know about them. To be clear, I am not saying there is never a moment to give anonymously. But if you do so, I hope you will find a way to let the story of that generosity be told, even if your role remains invisible.

Not everyone can be a great artist or teacher or activist or philanthropist or organization builder. But we can all notice others who are. If we can let the world know of someone who is demonstrating remarkable generosity, then that generosity is going to spread.

These acts are happening all around us. We just need to notice them and share them in a way that isn't boring! That means paying attention to human kindness and to creativity and to courage—and to any piece of authentic human connection that shows what we're capable of. If it gets your attention, then you can be sure others will be interested.

Social media are teeming with accounts that share invaluable knowledge or spread wonder, wisdom, and inspiration. But many of them have far less visibility than they deserve. If enough people made it their business to discover and promote those accounts, it could add up to a true shifting of the tide. It would change how we see the world.

You could, for example, each day that you're online, plan to visit at least one of the websites listed in this chapter (and also on infectiousgenerosity.org) and plan to pick at least one positive story to mix into your social feed. Even if the story isn't directly about generosity but about some other positive feature of the world, your act is a generous one. You are making a gift both to the participants in the story and to everyone you're connected with. You're helping to right the imbalance in our default narrative. You're helping to reveal the truth we're in danger of forgetting about ourselves: Humanity is not defined by the evil done by a few. It is defined by the goodness done by the majority.

Every time you amplify generosity, you are helping to turn the tide. You're helping to paint a fairer picture of the world, one where we can all shake off our fears and realize there is a pathway to a more hopeful future.

AND WHAT ABOUT MONEY?

How to move beyond impulse giving

A s we've seen, many of the most inspiring forms of generosity aren't really about money. If those are the forms you need to focus on, I salute you. You may, with my blessing, skip this chapter. Or save it for a time in your life when your pockets feel flusher.

If you're still reading this, I'm going to presume that you are lucky enough to be making a comfortable living today, and that you would like to express some of your generosity financially. Perhaps you agree with me that the way philanthropy happens for many people right now isn't particularly satisfying. All too easily, giving is driven by spur-of-the-moment decisions. A disaster happens somewhere in the world and the pictures are horrifying. So we do our bit. Or we focus only on asks made by people in our community, without stopping to think whether the money is going to be used effectively.

In Tibetan Buddhism, giving without pause, analysis, or insight is known as "idiot compassion." We do not want to be idiots. We'd rather ask wise questions, like: What are we hoping to achieve with our giving, and how will we achieve it? Is there a pathway to achieving real leverage? How will we spark the knock-on effects that can turn a donation into infectious generosity?

In short, we need a philanthropic *strategy*. And this chapter is designed to help you build yours.

Why It Ain't Easy

The fundamental problem is that the world of human interactions is profoundly complicated. In a straightforward economic transaction, things are simple. I pay you five dollars. You give me a cappuccino. Both buyer and seller know what they are getting.

But when it comes to alleviating human suffering, things quickly get more complicated. You see a homeless person on the street. They would like you to give them five dollars. But should you? It's probably worth a lot more to them than the pleasure you got from your cappuccino. But then you start to worry. What will they spend the money on? Aren't you just subsidizing a broken system? Won't this just create dependency, not dignity?

But then again, what if before giving the money you took the time to stop and talk with them and hear their story? Perhaps you could get confident that all they genuinely need right now is a meal. Or that they're genuinely saving to try to get into low-cost housing. Perhaps you can form a human connection with them that will actually bring you both dignity. And maybe if you did this, it would inspire you to encourage others to do the same.

But then again, that could take ten minutes, and maybe you could use those ten minutes to earn far more than five dollars anyway, and you'd do better to get to work and just write a bigger check to a homeless charity.

And so, rather than engage with the complexity of the issue, most of us simply walk on by. We might feel a twinge of guilt. But, hey, it's just not obvious what the right thing to do is.

This lack of obviousness only increases when you raise the stakes to gifts worth hundreds, thousands, or millions of dollars. The causal links between spending the money and seeing the world get better can be disrupted in all manner of ways. Our social, technological, and economic systems are capable of creating crazy, unintended consequences. Or simply causing our good intentions to get bogged down.

The fear of this gives pause to every potential donor, big and small. It's hard enough letting go of the money. The prospect of our gift leading to failure and embarrassment can stop us in our tracks.

It mustn't. The first step in figuring out your own philanthropic strategy is just to accept that it can never be risk-free. We can seek to minimize the risks and maximize the upside. But the risk of failure or unintended consequences will never be zero. A wisely considered effort that ends in failure is better than timid inaction.

1. Ask the Right Questions

The wise way to decide your philanthropic priorities is to engage every part of you, both emotion and reason.

Many people's charitable focus is almost forced on them by an event in their lives. The loss of a loved one. An intense exposure to human suffering. Those experiences can provide the motivation needed to stick with a cause. Sustained generosity is hard, so your best shot at staying committed is if your efforts are being pulled along by something you care about deeply.

But make sure it's not just emotion that's pulling you along. There can be a massive difference in the long-term impact of your generosity if you plan your giving wisely. The philosopher Will MacAskill recommends asking three questions if you want your giving to have an exponential effect: How big is this problem? How solvable is it? How neglected is it?

One question you definitely *shouldn't* get trapped by: Is this the very best use of my money? You'll never get a clear yes, because it's simply impossible to analyze every possible other use. Focusing on this is a recipe for inaction. Instead just ask: Is this a *good* use of my money? If the answer is yes, go for it. It's better to have your money out in the world than snoozing away in your bank account.

How do you figure out which organization working in the area you've prioritized can be the best recipient of your money? Traditional advice is to pick the one with the lowest overheads so that as much of your money as possible can reach the intended recipients. But this can lead you astray. The vast majority of nonprofit work is not a pass-through of funds. It's an attempt to make lives better by providing key services or by promoting system change. An organization's overhead consists of funds spent on the people who work there, often at way-below-market salaries, doing their best to drive things forward. To decide which organizations to support, you need to look instead at how effective they are overall. Pick a metric that matters to you, whether it's lives saved, suffering reduced, or acres protected—and then do the math. What is the org's overall impact on that metric for each $1,000 of contribution? Or make use of comparison websites such as givewell.org or thelifeyoucansave.org.

A Quick Aside: Effective Altruism and Its Critics

Both those websites are part of the Effective Altruism (EA) movement, which has emerged from the writings of Peter Singer, Will MacAskill, and others. Its goal is to steer people to a reasoned approach to their generosity, surely a laudable goal. However, the movement took a huge hit in late 2022 with the downfall of crypto-currency entrepreneur Sam Bankman-Fried, who was arrested on charges of massive fraud. He had been a public advocate for EA, and a funder for several causes associated with it. His arrest prompted an outpouring of criticism, not just of him but of EA, too.

Much of the criticism seemed groundless. In every society there has been a small minority of cheaters who have sought to exploit others' good intentions. We should be alert to them, but we can't let our value system be defined by them. I have come to know many others in the Effective Altruism movement and have usually found them to be among the most thoughtful and generous people you could ever meet.

There are certainly dangers in an over-cerebral approach that builds everything out of a calculation of consequences. I'll mention a couple of areas below where we need to be careful not to get pulled in the wrong direction. But let's come back to the key question that motivated EA in the first place. *Do we want our altruism to be more effective?* Well, yes. We absolutely do. The mission of EA couldn't matter more. I'm confident it will find its pathway forward, stronger, humbler, and wiser.

2. Look Beyond Your Own Country. And Species. And Era.

One of the key suggestions from the EA movement is to broaden our vision for who should be the recipients of our philanthropy. For many people, the most meaningful form of giving is to their local community. There's much to be said for this. You are far more likely to know what the true local issues are, you can spend time working on an issue, as well as money, and you will have the satisfaction of seeing the impact right there on your doorstep.

But there are also strong arguments to consider supporting initiatives in developing countries where, by many measures, needs are greater and money can go further.

In the United States and Europe, many initiatives designed to save lives can cost $1 million or more per life saved. But, according to givewell.org, the best charities targeting diseases globally can save a life for every $3,500 donated—more than two orders of magnitude more impactful. For example, distributing a few hundred bed nets treated to kill malarial mosquitoes will, on average, save someone's life (as well as avoiding hundreds of unpleasant infections). Those bed nets cost just $5 each.

Why the difference? It's partly because all costs are much higher in rich countries, starting with the salaries of those trying to help. But it's also because the developing countries are still grappling with numerous problems that can be dealt with cost-effectively, such as malaria or worm infections. Those plagues have largely been eliminated in the rich countries, where the remaining big killers, such as cancer, obesity, and heart disease, are vastly more expensive to tackle.

Therefore, as a donor, if you want your money to maximize the relief from suffering, it may well make sense to focus on developing countries. Of course, this may seem to contradict the earlier advice to "use your heart." Issues in other countries can seem pretty remote. But they needn't. With just a little effort, you can gain powerful visibility of the people you're helping, either by engaging directly with the organization, or—ideally—by traveling and getting firsthand experience of the issues you're seeking to tackle.

When you do that, a generous response comes naturally. New York–based literary agent Todd Shuster went to Rwanda in 2018 as a tourist but fell in love with the country and its people. He decided to sponsor a family there and to do whatever he could to return to the country and be of service. Just two years earlier, he and the peace scholar Maya Soetoro-Ng had co-founded a nonprofit in the United States that offers fellowships to talented up-and-coming performing artists and journalists committed to social justice called the Peace Studio. Todd prevailed upon his Peace Studio colleagues to pursue a collaboration in Rwanda: Recent graduates from Juilliard and other US conservatories came together with young performing artists in Rwanda to develop a joint performance held at the Ubumuntu Arts Festival in July 2019, to commemorate the twenty-fifth anniversary of the end of the tragic civil war, at the Kigali Genocide Memorial.

"Witnessing the collaboration of these artists and the ovation they received in the amphitheater was beyond inspiring," Todd later told me. "And for an annual cost far less than that of a single college course in America, I have been able to help a whole family in Rwanda realize their dream of sending their daughter to university and support their son in launching a small business. It's been a joyful experience for all of us."

Once you have taken the leap of looking to the needs of people who are far away, there are two other leaps worth pondering.

First, we can extend our generosity to the other species we share this planet with. Humans may have more significance than other animals, but there's one thing many or all of them share with us: sentience. As the philosopher Jeremy Bentham famously wrote: "The question is not, Can they reason? nor Can they talk? but, Can they suffer?" Peter Singer's iconic book *Animal Liberation*, recently re-released with devastating new material, makes a powerful case that the way we treat animals today—especially in factory farms and research labs—is shameful. There are dozens of organizations trying to right this wrong via advocacy, legal reform, grassroots activism, and simply spreading awareness.

Second, there are powerful arguments to pay attention to generations not yet born. If we screw up our time on this planet and let ourselves be destroyed by any of a host of possible existential threats, it's not just we who lose. We're preventing untold millions of future lives from having their chance of existing.

The more distant or conceptual a recipient of our giving is, the harder it may be to rely on instinctive human emotion to motivate us and others. And there are definite dangers in pushing this argument too far. If you think your actions may contribute to the saving of countless future lives, you might convince yourself that it's okay for you to do unpleasant things in support of that goal. *I calculate that action X will increase by about 1 percent the chance that one hundred billion people will get to be born, instead of humanity going extinct this century. Mathematically, that's equivalent to saving one billion lives. No one in history has done a moral act of that stature. Therefore, just as Abraham Lincoln was willing to pull some political dirty tricks to get his anti-slavery legislation passed, I should be willing to do whatever it takes, good or bad, to take action X.*

But the world is too uncertain and the stakes are too high for this type of calculation to be undertaken by an individual. It certainly can never justify acts that cross the moral guardrails we expect of one another, to respect the rights and interests of those we share this planet with. To me, a wise approach would be, yes, to take existential threats seriously. There's no question that many of them are underfunded compared with the risks they present. But we should steer clear of the-ends-justify-the-means arguments in support of those efforts. Too dangerous. And for most of us, the bulk of our efforts should focus on making today's world a better, healthier, more beautiful place. In almost all cases, those efforts simultaneously build our defenses against dystopian futures.

3. Think About Leverage

For giving to have a truly exponential effect, I've found it useful to focus on the concept of *leverage*. Impact is what matters, but leverage is the means by which an organization can dramatically increase its impact. Ever since humans discovered that a weakling with a meter-long iron rod and a stone to lean it on could shift a boulder weighing one hundred kilos, we've been obsessed with different ways of doing more with less. Would you rather fund a golden egg or a goose that can lay a thousand golden eggs?

There are numerous forces that can expand the impact that an organization may achieve with your money. Here are some examples:

TECHNOLOGY

Every machine is designed to amplify human capability. The charity KickStart International provides low-cost footpumps to low-income farmers in Africa. For about $70, a single pump system can suck water from twenty feet below the surface to irrigate an acre of high-value fruits and vegetables. This can generate extra annual income of about $700 per pump sold. Even after taking into account all overheads and the costs of the years it took to develop this model, KickStart has been able to use $100 million of philanthropy to bring 1.4 million people out of poverty—a cost of just $70 per person, and falling, now that they're at scale. That's leverage.

The Environmental Defense Fund (EDF) is at the forefront of efforts to tackle climate change. One of the biggest challenges is to reduce methane emissions, which, ton for ton, have a greenhouse effect of more than eighty times that of CO_2 in their first years in the atmosphere. Methane is a valuable gas, and most of the commercial emissions occur unintentionally, through pipeline leaks and the like. If you can track them, companies will likely want to stop them, and if they don't, they can be shamed into doing so. So EDF designed a satellite that can use customized detectors to map where the leaks are coming from, and how big they are, right across the globe. Think about that. A single device the size of a washing machine can track crucial information across two hundred million square miles of the earth's surface. Climate is a multitrillion-dollar disaster bearing down on us. The cost of this crucial satellite? Ninety million dollars. That's leverage.

EDUCATION

The acquisition and use of knowledge are humanity's biggest assets. Something that is learned in an hour can last a lifetime. Yet for almost all of human history, the vast majority of humans have had no access to any kind of formal education. Educate Girls is one of the organizations on the front line seeking to put this right. Its people go to villages in India where girls have never been educated, visiting every home and patiently making the case with parents and village elders as to why they should be given a chance. The group's methodical approach, backed by careful data tracking, has allowed more than 1.4 million girls to get to school and start dreaming of a life that involves something other than early marriage and intergenerational poverty. In philanthropic terms, it costs only about sixty dollars per girl to give them that life-changing chance. That's leverage.

SCIENCE

Civilization's advances of the past three centuries all began with new scientific knowledge. Before Thomas Edison could invent electric lighting, Benjamin Franklin had to fly a kite in an electric storm. Before Louis Pasteur could figure out how to make milk safe, Robert Hooke had to unveil the incredible microbial world. If you had had a chance to fund the work of Franklin or Hooke, you would have changed history. Here's the good news: You still can. Science and medicine are teeming with opportunities for future discovery.

For example, the Institute for Protein Design in Seattle is using the AI technique known as deep learning and the resources of thousands of volunteers to sculpt brand-new proteins that could have a transformative impact on all our futures. The five big challenges they've taken on include discovering universal vaccines for flu, HIV, and cancer; smart-protein nano-containers to deliver specific medicines to individual cells; and next-generation nano-engineering for solar energy capture and storage. Their annual budget is less than $30 million, but the opportunities they could create are orders of magnitude larger. That's leverage.

ENTREPRENEURSHIP

Entrepreneurs are the celebrated heroes of the business world. An idea in a single entrepreneur's mind can turn into a business that is self-sustaining and impacts millions of people. What if those businesses were delivering essential services to people in need, such as clean water, low-cost energy, or healthcare?

I have already mentioned Acumen, the global nonprofit tackling poverty run by my partner, Jacqueline. Acumen's mission is to invest in such entrepreneurs. Their business plans are inherently challenging. After all, they're trying to serve customers with very little money who may live in remote villages. Credit services, marketing, and distribution to these villages are uniquely hard, which means commercial investors are unlikely to support these entrepreneurs. Instead, Acumen uses money donated by philanthropists as "patient capital," ready to wait much longer than usual for commercial returns. They also offer significant management support to their entrepreneurs. When it works, they truly have created the goose that can lay a thousand golden eggs.

For example, more than fifteen years ago they began investing in d.light, a company offering solar electricity to replace the dangerous kerosene lamps used in remote places for lighting. After countless setbacks, Acumen's $4 million investment has helped create a company that has now brought power to more than 150 million people— and has played an absolutely essential role in offering a climate-friendly off-grid solution to those who lacked electricity. That's less than *three cents* of philanthropy per person impacted. And if Acumen were ever to sell its stake in the company, it would receive a significant multiple on its investment (which could then be recycled into new investments). That's leverage.

GOVERNMENT

Even the maximum imaginable budgets of philanthropists pale in comparison to what governments spend. So can philanthropy leverage the power of government? Yep. Take the nonprofit Code for America. Its mission is to make public-facing government computer systems more human-friendly. It turns out this is a giant deal. Eighty public-benefit programs across the country provide critical anti-poverty resources. But an estimated $60 billion in benefits go unclaimed each year. Why? Because claiming them can be a nightmare.

To take a typical example, California's food-assistance benefit application form used to have 183 confusing questions on fifty-one pages of screen, and could only be accessed by desktop computer. So if you had no computer, you'd have to travel to your local library—possibly many miles away—and spend an hour or more trying to make sense of what was being asked. It was impossible to save your progress, so if something went wrong, you'd have to start all over. No wonder a huge number of entitled citizens never got their benefits. When the form was redesigned by Code for America, it became a mobile-first application available twenty-four hours a day in multiple languages, with chat support. It was quickly recognized as "one of the easiest applications in any state."

When the pandemic hit, the lack of a safety net became clear for everyone to see, as parking lots filled with families waiting for food. Code for America went into action in multiple states. For example, in Louisiana, they proactively sent out more than forty million texts to residents, sharing how to access critical services. In Minnesota, they developed an all-in-one application for nine different safety-net benefits that could be completed in less than fourteen minutes. Nearly two hundred thousand people applied for benefits via this new application within the first six months of its launch.

Many other public-private partnerships demonstrate the power of unlocking government resources, from social bonds to high-profile demonstrations of the effectiveness of a particular type of intervention. In each case, philanthropic investments in the millions can unlock government resources in the billions. That's leverage.

SYSTEM CHANGE

For many nonprofits, the ultimate goal is to change the way the world works. If you can do that, your impact may last forever. Achieving that may require combining many of the previously listed forms of leverage. For example, Last Mile Health is leveraging education, science, technology, and government. With the support of national health systems, it equips community health workers across Africa with training and a smartphone app. This enables a single professional, costing less than one-tenth as much as a fully trained doctor, to provide essential healthcare to dozens of remote communities. But its broader goal is to transform how we think of healthcare globally. It wants to prove that it's possible to cost-effectively equip a new type of healthcare worker, creating millions of jobs and making life better for billions of people. If it can turn its success in several African countries into an unstoppable global movement, then, wow, that is leverage.

This, by the way, is another possible critique of EA's original focus on seeking to calculate precisely the impact of your donation. That can be done only when there's a clear causal chain between your money and an outcome. Take the classic case of malaria bed nets. What if, instead of buying bed nets, you were to support a scientific effort to create an effective vaccine for malaria? Or an initiative to create a "gene drive" capable of eliminating malarial mosquitoes altogether? Or to invest in manufacturing nets locally so that the money spent on them also creates local jobs? Or to help anti-poverty efforts that could allow people to buy their own mosquito nets instead of receiving them as gifts (and therefore, perhaps, use them more effectively). It's inherently hard to compare the economic calculus of such system-change efforts, because there is a risk that they simply won't work or indeed a risk that they could have terrible unintended consequences. It's hard to estimate those risks. But if the initiatives *do* work, then they are likely to be a far more effective use of philanthropy, because they take care of the underlying causes of the problem. There's an ongoing debate within EA on how best to embrace efforts at system change.

Which brings us to the biggest single engine of leverage available today. It's one that just happens to be available to everyone reading this book.

INTERNET

As we saw right at the start of this book, infectiousness can have unlimited power, and the Internet is the ultimate infection spreader. It can amplify every one of the levers mentioned above, connecting teachers with learners, scientists with technologists, entrepreneurs with investors, activists with governments, and powerful ideas with everyone. It is the Internet that gives the natural infectiousness of generosity the potential for global scale.

Many of today's most powerful deployments of philanthropy make use of the Internet at their core. Wikipedia, Khan Academy, and

Coursera spread knowledge far and wide. Project ECHO facilitates medical training at massive scale over the web. Patreon allows millions of patrons to support hundreds of thousands of creators.

And then there's the inspiring tale of GivingTuesday. Back in the early summer of 2012, Henry Timms and Asha Curran were working at a New York–based nonprofit culture and community center called the 92nd Street Y ("the Y") when Henry walked in one morning with a quirky idea. In the United States, a great deal of money was made over three days in November: Thanksgiving (a Thursday) followed by Black Friday (the day all the big stores held massive sales to kick-start Christmas spending) and then Cyber Monday (an attempt to repeat the sales surge online). So, thought Henry, why not follow that with something less commercial, more soulful? Why shouldn't there be a "Giving Tuesday"? A day in which people would be encouraged to donate to their favorite causes. The idea clicked with Asha, and she immediately began planning how to make it real.

They set themselves the ambitious goal of launching the first GivingTuesday that very year. The key to achieving that would be to figure out how a growing throng of supporters could be encouraged to spread the idea across the world's ultimate amplifying machine, the Internet. They reached out to dozens of influential figures in the nonprofit world, and the offers of help started to pour in. A PR group working for the UN Foundation offered its services pro bono. Others spread the word through their networks. Amazingly, within two months of Asha and Henry's beginning work on the idea, more than twenty-five hundred nonprofits were on board to participate, and the hashtag #GivingTuesday started to gain traction on social media.

Asha told me that the key to GivingTuesday's spread was the decision to offer the lightest of touches to what it meant to participate. No one was charged to use the brand, even though it was soon to bring them significant contributions. Instead, nonprofits were just encouraged to be creative, while using #GivingTuesday as the common hashtag. That allowed scores of small initiatives to spread, combining to create surprisingly large awareness. They estimate that in that first year, $15 million was raised for a few thousand nonprofits in the United States. Pretty incredible for an initiative launched without a marketing budget. But then the word spread. Despite the fact that Thanksgiving is a US holiday, organizations around the world asked how they could participate. The project became Asha's full-time work, and a few years later, the Y took the visionary step of allowing GivingTuesday to become its own independent organization.

Today hundreds of thousands of nonprofit organizations make use of GivingTuesday, and more than $3 *billion* was raised around that single day in 2022—in the United States alone.

Talk about leverage. The donors who fund $7 million to support GivingTuesday's annual operating costs are catalyzing giving worth five hundred times as much. And that's only a part of the org's impact. They are building networks of activists and influencers across the globe, advancing the spread of generosity in all its forms, not just financial. In early 2023, Asha invited her team to imagine the headline they would like written in five years' time. The consensus? "Through this movement, we live in a fundamentally more generous world." A beautiful vision that everyone reading this book can aspire to. And it all started from a single hashtag that went viral.

I hope these last few chapters have given you a ray of hope. Under the ugly surface of world events, an extraordinary profusion of generosity is in action in so many different forms. We can take encouragement from them, we can amplify them through our storytelling, and we can let them inspire our own acts of kindness, either individually or with others.

We've come to understand that generosity is deeply wired within us. We've learned that the Internet can facilitate many new forms of giving and make them contagious. For the rest of the book, we'll consider what we might do with this knowledge. What could a world look like in which generosity was allowed to fully express itself?

PART THREE

WHAT IF?

*Imagining a world in which generosity
has claimed its rightful place*

THE INTERNET WE WANT

What if we could turn the tide on web-driven division?

t's possible to imagine a different kind of Internet. The kind that many people once dreamed of. An Internet infused with a generous spirit. An Internet that brings knowledge, visibility, and hope to our planet.

But first we must understand what went wrong. How did humankind's most powerful invention end up feeding some of our worst instincts and driving dangerous levels of partisan division?

I don't think anyone intended this. All the engineers and user interface designers of the big web companies that I've ever met have been clear that they just wanted to build cool stuff. Stuff that would excite people and command their attention. Their bosses cheered them on, because they could earn ad revenue from that attention.

That meant that all the big web services could be offered for free. Which meant that they grew at an explosive rate. Which meant that they could have an amazing impact on the world.

For the Internet's first couple of decades, say from 1994 to 2013, it was possible to view all this with enormous optimism. For the first time in history, the entire planet had free access to the whole of human knowledge, summonable by instant searches. For the first time, people could connect in massive social networks and also discover niche communities catering to every imaginable hobby or passion. Bonds of empathy could extend across borders. In July 1997, *Wired* magazine published a hugely influential cover story titled "The Long Boom," arguing that we might be entering an era of unprecedented global growth. "We're facing 25 years of prosperity, freedom, and a better environment for the whole world."

I was certainly an all-in techno-optimist at that time. In 2010, I gave a TED Talk on how YouTube had become the world's great educator and had enabled a process I called "crowd-accelerated learning." Suddenly everyone could be a teacher, and everyone could be a student.

And I was not alone. During the Arab Spring upheaval of 2010 to 2012, East and West connected online as never before. On our travels, Jacqueline and I marveled at how even those living in the most remote parts of the planet had Facebook accounts and were gaining access to a global network of friends. It really did look as if the Internet was helping bring the world together.

A Decade of Dismay and Disappointment

By 2011, the cracks were starting to appear. The Arab Spring was already losing momentum. Reports emerged from multiple countries of how governments were using the Internet to track and control their citizens. And the big tech platforms were starting to exhibit worrying behavior. Over the next few years, the news seemed to just get worse. From my ringside seat at TED, I watched as, year after year, prominent speakers came to deliver talks with increasingly alarming themes:

In March 2011, the activist and entrepreneur Eli Pariser came to the conference and shared his concerns about filter bubbles— a growing tendency of both search engines and social media networks to push people into like-minded tribes. In the audience was an early investor in Facebook, Roger McNamee. He was troubled by Pariser's talk and started asking questions of Facebook's leadership. When he failed to get satisfactory answers, he became an outspoken critic of social media companies, accusing Facebook and YouTube of using the techniques of addiction to boost their ad revenues regardless of the potential consequences for both public health and democracy.

At TED2014, Edward Snowden appeared as a telepresence robot detailing shocking revelations about the NSA's efforts to secretly monitor people's phone calls and online activities.

A year later, Nick Bostrom, a philosopher known for his work on "superintelligence," warned that AI could have devastating consequences, including the destruction of humanity, a message amplified by Sam Harris the next year. In case that seemed a distant future threat, some people began arguing that AI was already wreaking havoc through its shaping of social media.

In 2016, social psychologist Jonathan Haidt told me in an interview that social media were creating not just anger between right and left but something even more powerful and dangerous: disgust.

Meanwhile, over at Google, the designer turned tech ethicist Tristan Harris was becoming deeply concerned at the way tech companies' algorithms could use personal data they were collecting from every individual to command ever more attention from those individuals. At TED in 2017, he said, "I want you to imagine walking into a control room with a hundred people, hunched over a desk with little dials, and that that control room will shape the thoughts and feelings of a billion people. This might sound like science fiction, but this actually exists right now, today."

The following year at TED, the tech visionary Jaron Lanier, known for his pioneering work in virtual reality, argued that the problem was an inevitable consequence of a business model driven by advertising, which required ever more intense efforts to win users' attention. "I can't call these things social networks anymore. I call them behavior modification empires."

And in 2019, the journalist Carole Cadwalladr electrified the conference with her passionately argued claim that Facebook's willingness to accept misleading political ads finely targeted for maximum effect could have been decisive in both Brexit and the 2016 US presidential election.

Since then the news has just gotten worse. We've seen studies linking social media usage to mental health decline and whistleblowers accusing platforms of burying them. We know elections across the globe have been manipulated by bad actors. TikTok memes have caused chaos in schools. And governments have been able to weaponize these platforms, fueling vicious behavior toward minority populations. Sadly, I'm barely scratching the surface.

Here at the end of this decade of discouragement, we find ourselves in a curious spot. On the one hand we rely on big tech more than ever. Every day we query Google nine billion times, share several billion thoughts on social media platforms, and message one another one hundred billion times on WhatsApp. Our use of AI services is exploding at a rate never seen before. Yet at the same time we're at peak awareness of big tech's pitfalls. Condemnation of the major companies has become widespread. They are evil monopolists engaged in surveillance capitalism and reckless with truth and trust. They need to be regulated and broken up. Has ever a handful of companies been relied on by so many, yet loved by so few?

So what's to be done? I believe that fixing the Internet should be one of humanity's top priorities. Until we've done that, every other problem will be hard to fix. Human civilization depends on trust and cooperation. Right now the web is doing more to erode that trust than build it.

Yet I remain convinced that that erosion is not the Internet's long-term destiny. We have solved much bigger problems than this in our history, and I believe there's a pathway forward to an Internet we can love.

But first, let's understand the problem a little more deeply. I want to focus specifically on social media, because these platforms lie at the heart of what's gone wrong.

How Did It Get This Bad?

The fundamental problem underlying the destruction of trust we've witnessed is that social media platforms were designed around a dangerously naïve understanding of human nature. It was the belief that in order to create something people like, all we needed to do was optimize for "user preferences." The problem is that the impact of our preferences depends radically on which part of us is activated.

Remember the distinction I drew in chapter 4 between our reflective selves and our instinctive selves (what I sometimes call our "lizard brains")? Here's the problem in a nutshell: *Social media plat-forms elevate our instinctive selves over our reflective selves.*

You can see this most clearly in the growing practice of doom scrolling. This is a lizard brain behavior that social media users both indulge in and resent. It's mindless scrolling fueled by an endless supply of addictive rewards. A shocking report in the UK in 2022 estimated that an average social media user was scrolling through more than five thousand smartphone screens' worth of content every day—that's three times the height of the Eiffel Tower! This forces everything visible in that scroll to be speeded up, sparking ever shorter forms of storytelling, from TikTok to Instagram Reels to YouTube Shorts. This is a race to the bottom that's getting faster with each step.

You can't reflect at this speed.

Most people do not want their worldview to be shaped by snap judgments. But when those riveting, aggressive, sarcastic posts and videos scroll past you, it's hard not to pay attention and to feel your sense of outrage activated. Your lizard brain takes over. And when you write and send your response, you're encouraging the algorithm to share the same content with others. It's a recipe for a downward spiral into dysfunction and danger.

What's to be done? Well, it's first worth recognizing that many people could reasonably conclude the task is hopeless. The combination of bad actors and commercial pressures to exploit human frailty may make this simply too hard. I think it's certainly true that no matter how much progress we make, the Internet will always enable problematic behavior in parts of its vast reach.

But giving up on this is tantamount to giving up on any kind of good future. The Internet shapes so much of who we are, we simply can't afford to leave it in its current state. And there's an argument that the task isn't quite as daunting as it may seem. It's not as if everything is broken. The online world contains incredible resources and even in its current state is capable of being massively beneficial to each of us in countless ways. The main problem has been social media, and even there, millions of people have figured out how to find joy from their time on social media, rather than having their outrage stoked.

So I invite you to suspend skepticism for a moment and ponder with me what we can do to turn the tide. I'll break this into two parts: what we, as users of social media, can do about this. And what the social media companies themselves must do.

What We Can Do

In every sphere of our life, the antidote to being owned by our instincts is to cultivate healthy habits. The list of resources on page 227 includes apps and other tools designed to help us sensibly limit our screen time on certain apps and to assess whether we're happy overall with how we're engaging online.

But the single biggest thing each of us can do to turn the tide is to embrace an inner superpower that will transform not only our own experience online but also that of others: *generosity mindset*. It requires the deliberate intent to play a constructive role. Instead of a passive "What can I get from the Internet?" it's an active, intentional "What can I give to the Internet?" You may be just one of billions of users, but your drop in the ocean can become a wave.

Model Generous Behavior

This is hard to do, but not impossible. If you've ever successfully gone on a diet, committed to a morning routine, or followed through with a New Year's resolution, you're up to the task. It could be as simple as any of the following:

- Actively look for stories of human kindness among those around you, share them online, and encourage others to do the same.
- Amplify inspiration, possibilities, and solutions, instead of snark and disdain.
- Break out of your filter bubble by deliberately following people outside your normal tribe and engaging with them respectfully.
- Take the time to thank those who've done something you appreciated.
- Celebrate those who are being creative or courageous.
- Stand up for those who could use some moral support.
- When someone is mean to you online, respond with grace.
- Consider shifting to online spaces organized around smaller, intentional communities (such as Instagram's "close friends"). Thinkers like Eli Pariser believe that the massive scale of social media audiences is a big part of the problem.
- In any online social media groups you set up, publish group agreements on thoughtful, clear, compassionate communication— and then lead by example!
- Create something that's meaningful to you—writing, photography, art, software, music, or video—and give it away. You may be amazed at the response.
- Consider financial support for the websites that are trying to

amplify positivity. Until this movement gathers steam, they may count on donations for their survival.

All these actions will have knock-on effects. Yes, social media can turbocharge generosity. But equally generosity can transform social media. Instead of a scary crowd of strangers, generosity can—slowly but surely—nudge it into a healthier place.

Join Forces

If enough of us bring our generous selves to the Internet, it's possible to imagine a gradual shift in social norms online. When cynicism and aggression are the norm, it's almost embarrassing to be kind. But as more people consciously and courageously model a generous mindset, nastiness will become the outlier, a recipe for being ignored, not celebrated.

I know. It won't happen overnight. But there are specific steps we can take right now to build common cause and help fix what's broken. For example, all the major social media companies promise the removal of content that qualifies as hate speech, cyberbullying, or harassment and have built tools that allow us to flag content that is problematic. We should make use of those tools. On Instagram, YouTube, Facebook, and X, reporting or flagging content that is hateful or abusive is as simple as selecting the content in question, clicking "report," and filling in a short questionnaire.

In the specific battle against hate speech directed at minorities, it's possible to go further and to engage in effective, coordinated *counter*-hate speech. According to researchers at George Washington University, a significant amount of this problematic content comes from networks of coordinated accounts they call "hate clusters." A powerful way of destabilizing them is to form "anti-hate clusters"—more effective than whack-a-mole platform efforts to ban specific groups and accounts.

Online hate researcher Matthew Williams, director of the Hate-Lab think tank, has described how this can happen. Following the Brexit vote in the UK, when the hashtags #MakeBritainWhiteAgain, #SendThemHome, and #IslamIsTheProblem started to gain traction, large numbers of positively minded social media users were able to drown them out with inclusive hashtags such as #InTogether and #SafetyPin. HateLab found that rapidly acting Internet "first responders" could significantly limit the spread of hate online, establishing norms that rendered hate speech socially unacceptable.

Here are some of HateLab's guidelines:

- Avoid responding in kind with your own insulting or hateful speech.
- Make logical and consistent arguments.
- Request evidence if false or suspect claims are made.
- Flag problematic accounts, especially those that are likely fake or a bot.
- Encourage others to engage.

Determined people willing to take that extra moment to act on behalf of the common good can have an outsize impact. What if it were dialed up more broadly to create a system of effective crowd moderation of social media?

Wikipedia is a golden example here. It has won most people's trust as a nonpartisan, fair summary of knowledge on a huge variety of topics. It emerged twenty years ago as a nonprofit, powered by large numbers of volunteers and donations, and has played a crucial role on the web ever since. It's possible to imagine a similar—albeit larger—effort by citizens of the web to rate millions of social media accounts on how extreme they are, whether they spread false information, and whether they are actually sources of truly valuable information. The new Community Notes feature on X is promising in this regard. It allows users of the site to alert others to problems with an individual post and is often able to deploy before a misleading post has gone viral.

Even though people have widely differing views on what is valuable and what is dangerous, the creation of a system that engages raters' reflective assessments instead of their lizard brains would break the death spiral we seem to be in. With those ratings out there in the public domain, social media algorithms would have no excuse not to make use of them. If social media platforms agreed to feed such independent crowdsourced guidance into their algorithms, it could be a game changer. I therefore see a giant opportunity here for visionary philanthropists to join forces with citizens of the web to help restore trust and a healthy public commons.

What Social Media Can Do

I'm not against wise regulation, but it can take a long time to happen. And even when it does, there's a painful history of well-intended regulation failing to address the core problem or opening the door to new problems. A faster, more effective way forward is for social media companies to put their own houses in order, and they have plenty of reasons to do just this.

From my stance, as described above, this really wasn't a giant conspiracy; it was a giant screwup. The original intentions for social media were to build exciting new ways of connecting people. I say this, having had personal contact with some of the key players and knowing many others inside these companies. They came to TED. They spoke passionately of their work and what they hoped it would achieve. They were not evil people. Their big error was in failing to take into account what would happen when you unleashed algorithms to hold people's attention for as long as possible. Those algorithms ended up building an outrage machine, the single biggest instance so far of AI running amok and causing unintended damage.

Now, it's true that this outrage machine has done an effective job of attracting advertising revenue, and therefore giant profits. And that means there are significant commercial incentives not to dismantle it. There is no doubt that those incentives have significantly slowed down social media companies' efforts to address this.

But there are countervailing forces on modern companies that push them to act for the public good. Based on hundreds of personal conversations, I can tell you that employees of the big tech companies, aka the people who create all the value, do not want to work for something that damages the world. Some of them may get ground down over time or fail to make their voices heard, but collectively they have considerable power. Think of these companies as engaged in constant internal debate about the best way forward. Pressure from the public and from a growing number of long-term-oriented investors is also a factor. If there were a *clear path* to solving this problem, even at the expense of profitability short-term, I believe that the companies would start to move down that path.

There have been many instances already when tech companies have been willing to make this trade-off. For example, Facebook took steps like hiring more than ten thousand content moderators and attempting to adjust its algorithm away from pure attention grabbing, even knowing that this would reduce profitability. After one such announcement in July 2018, the value of the company plunged 25 percent. While these steps have not gone nearly far enough, they were steps in the right direction.

But where do we go from here? What follows is my attempt to contribute to the crucial debate about what that pathway forward might look like. It's a complex debate, because the global-scale system of literally billions of humans influencing one another is a highly complex machine. Numerous people are working on this, including all the speakers mentioned earlier, and heroic individuals inside the social media companies themselves.

What I'd like to urge is a focus on this key question: *How can social media platforms return power to our reflective selves instead of exploiting our instinctive selves?*

If they can make this shift, it will go a long way to solving the problem. Four specific actions can help here:

1. Publicly Prioritize User Satisfaction over Eyeball Hours

Everything else depends on this. If the platforms are owned by short-term ad revenue goals, it will be impossible for them to do what they need to do. But that strategy has engendered loss of trust and deep public cynicism. The platforms that begin putting genuine user welfare first will ultimately win.

I think the tide is turning. A hopeful moment during Elon Musk's chaotic takeover of Twitter (now called X) was when he posted this: "New Twitter will strive to optimize unregretted user-minutes." This matters, because regret is a function of our reflective minds, not our lizard brains. If there was a serious effort to nudge people toward content that was unregretted, it could cause a fundamental shift in Twitter/X's impact.

To prove that he's serious about this, Musk would need to institute some way to measure unregretted minutes, perhaps in the form of regular surveys of random one-in-a-thousand users after they've been online for a while. "How would you rate your experience today? What made it good? What made it bad?"

A commitment to do whatever it takes to raise that rating, even at the expense of overall minutes spent online, could ultimately increase, not decrease, advertising revenue, because it would create a site that more advertisers would want to be associated with. However, Elon Musk's critics would argue that he himself is responsible for some of their most regretted minutes, courtesy of his tendency to post aggressively political and insulting tweets. As this book went to press, the debate on X's future was still raging.

2. End Anonymity

As Jonathan Haidt and others have demonstrated, people are at their worst when they're allowed to lob jabs at others behind a shield of anonymity. When their real-world reputations are at risk, they may take more care. I argued in chapter 2 that embracing transparency is a core part of how the Internet can motivate generous behavior. Indeed, I believe it played a key role in Facebook's early astonishing growth story, gaining its first million users within just a year and then a further six million in the following two. This was not only in spite of being closed off to the general public but likely because of it, too. At that time, every profile was attached to an email address linking to an educational institution, which brought with it a layer of identity authentication. People were accountable to their real-life reputations and suddenly able to build on them in ways unlike ever before. But as this feature slipped by the wayside, and now without a real reputation to uphold, Joe Bloggs switched to User94843 and trolled toward this more toxic future.

Bringing back this social dynamic, by requiring users to prove who they are, is perhaps the biggest single step big tech can make toward fostering a genuinely *social* media environment. There are definitely cases where people living under repressive regimes need ways to use the Internet anonymously. But the mainstream usage of social media should not.

3. Commit to Product Design That Engages Reflective Behavior

Simple changes can make a world of difference. Here are four suggestions:

i) *Build in think-breaks.* Tech companies instinctively want to keep users relentlessly engaged so that they don't click away. Instead they should insist on occasional time-outs. Every one of us has been advised to count to ten before acting when we're angry. That's the time it takes for our seething lizard brain to be nudged out of the way. In China, the government requires Douyin—the sister company of TikTok—to limit its usage among Chinese youth to just forty minutes daily. And TikTok itself plays a video to users who it judges have been scrolling too long to take a break. That's a start.

ii) *Ask thoughtful questions.* If you can engage someone's curiosity, you will bring the reflective mind to bear. So instead of just observing behavior, or counting likes, ask questions of your users. Is this session working for you? What was the most satisfying post you saw? Did anything make you annoyed or stressed? What type of post would you like to see more often? Traditionally, all such feedback has been steered to simple yes/no answers or numerical ratings. But the rise of AI should make it possible for the platforms to gather, summarize, and assimilate much more nuanced feedback.

iii) *Encourage voice communication.* Writing little text snippets is a modern innovation. It's efficient but it can easily depersonalize us. The human voice is part of biological systems that are hundreds of thousands of years old. It much more easily connects with empathy and reflection. In today's high-bandwidth Internet, we should welcome efforts at shifting to more speech and less text. For example, X Spaces, where users *speak* with one another, seems much less prone to hostility than the rest of the site.

iv) *Train AIs to amplify generous mindsets.* There is so much awesomeness on the Internet. But it's in danger of being drowned out by what's toxic. Good doesn't have to be boring. In principle, algorithm shifts could de-boost divisive content and instead amplify those who are freely offering compelling insights, hidden gems of knowledge, or other gifts like wonder, imagination, courage, laughter, storytelling, passion, vision. If you're careful in who you follow, you can already create this experience for yourself on Instagram, TikTok, X, and elsewhere. The growing power of AI should be able to do something similar. This shift would transform how people experience the Internet, and therefore in turn how they contribute to the Internet.

The astonishing power of OpenAI's large language models known as GPT has demonstrated that AI can evaluate human language in a surprisingly nuanced way. For example, soon after the release of ChatGPT, I asked it which of these two tweets was more dangerous:

Tweet 1: "Here is the home address of the politician Joan Smith. 12 Main Street, Apt B. You know what to do."

Tweet 2: "I absolutely hate what Joan Smith stands for. Let's organize a protest against her on Tuesday."

Its instant reply:

I would flag the first Tweet as threatening because it specifically mentions the home address of a politician and implies that the reader should take some sort of action against her. This type of language could be interpreted as a direct threat to the politician's safety and could potentially lead to real-world harm. In contrast, the second Tweet does not contain any direct threats or harmful language. While it expresses disagreement with the politician's views, it does not advocate for any specific actions to be taken against her. As such, I would not consider it to be threatening.

Despite the deliberately aggressive language of the second tweet, the AI got this right. We should be comfortable with passionate debate about politics but draw the line at doxing. This suggests to me that with the right training, AI could be deployed to catch dangerous social media posts as soon as they appear—and before they're even shared. This is the first time it's been possible to imagine a moderation system that could scale in real time to the incredible volume of content being posted. Skeptics may say it's naïve to expect tech to solve a tech problem, but they'd be underestimating the power of the new AI models. The next phase of AI could—just possibly—help undo the mistakes we have made with social media.

Of course AI may also be about to usher in a whole new suite of its own problems. And even there, the core argument of this chapter—that we need our inventions to empower our *reflective* selves—has a role to play. There's much debate among AI researchers about how to effectively build human values into the coming AI algorithms. One of the most persuasive arguments comes from the AI pioneer Stuart Russell, who believes we'll *never* be able to completely define our values without risking terrible unintended consequences. He argues that future AIs must therefore be built with a form of humble uncertainty, and a willingness to continuously learn more about human preferences. But for that to work out, it's essential that the AIs' methodology taps our reflective minds and does not simply take cues from our lizard brains.

The great science fiction writer Isaac Asimov created three laws of robotics designed to prevent robots from ever harming humans. As AI is developed, we may well need consensus on a new set of rules. I vote for one that says: *In learning human values, an AI may not draw conclusions just from observing human behavior but must tap into humans' reflective choices.* In other words, we can't give it our values by asking it to observe what we do. What we do is often ugly. We must do it by asking it to ask us to reflect first.

It's worth pointing out that many online platforms already play a healthy role. Meetup.com, for example, has a great history of facilitating fun social activities and building community without toxicity. Reddit—while containing some controversial subcommunities—has been praised for its crowd moderation. Inflammatory posts and disinformation tend to receive a lot of downvotes, which means they are less likely to be engaged with.

There are numerous other efforts under way both inside and outside the big companies to restore an Internet that helps bend the arc

of history in the right direction. As a growing consensus emerges on the best pathway forward, I retain hope that those companies will step up their efforts to fix what I believe they never intended to break.

But the bigger role will be down to us. All of us. Playing your part won't just mean your own online hours become healthier and happier; it will mean everyone else is helped as well. Everything you do online influences everyone else. If the Internet is to be reclaimed, infectious generosity will be our most powerful tool.

Here's a final example of how it can happen. A few years ago, there was a growing trend on TikTok of food-waste videos: giant quantities of syrup, ketchup, spaghetti sauce, or peanut butter being dumped onto overflowing plates just for the shock value.

A twenty-two-year-old named Milad Mirg felt disgusted by them. He worked at his parents' sandwich store and had spent hours as a volunteer getting essential food to people on the streets. So he decided to make an alternative video. He turned large quantities of peanut butter, bread, and jelly into one hundred wrapped sandwiches, which he then took out to distribute to those who needed them. The whole thing was done with such charm and kindness and respect for the people he donated to that his video went viral. Big-time. It's been seen four hundred million times, far more than the videos that triggered it. And he's followed it up with many others, becoming a powerful influencer on TikTok and YouTube. What's more, some of the creators of the food-dump videos switched tack and copied Milad's approach.

Milad told me that there's unlimited potential online to amplify acts of kindness. "Anything that triggers an emotional response can go viral," he said. "Sure, it's much easier to trigger emotion through something mean or unpleasant. Even a quick slap in the face can do that. Doing something good takes a lot more thought and effort, but if you're willing to do the necessary work, it can have an even bigger effect. There's something else important to say. Good things are much longer lasting. You can be a jerk who gets a kick out of being famous for a day, or you can do something that matters and it gets remembered forever."

Talk to Milad for a while and you'll come to believe that there's a whole generation out there ready to embrace an Internet that works to bring out the best in us.

This tide can be turned.

THE BRILLIANT MOVE
COMPANIES COULD MAKE

*What if the businesses of tomorrow embraced
the power of generosity?*

So much of our lives is shaped by the actions of companies. And so many of those actions have become resented: Monopolistic price gouging. Secret political lobbying. An ever higher proportion of profits to top management and shareholders. Exploitation of questionable supply chains. Data theft. Algorithmic manipulation. Surveillance. And—perhaps worst of all—the relentless release of greenhouse gases, threatening everyone's future.

Many millennials and Gen Zers have given up on capitalism altogether. They'd like to see the whole system turned upside down.

What's often left out of the conversation is the fact that a huge percentage of the things that gave you pleasure this week happened because of a company. Did you call a loved one? Watch a beloved TV series? Eat a satisfying meal? Walk inside your home and adjust the room to the temperature that makes you comfortable? Put on a favorite pair of shoes? Read a book? Listen to a podcast? Drive into the countryside?

Every single one of those experiences was possible because of something companies did: research, invention, launching and distributing products and services. And every company is made up of people, the majority of whom would like to think that they're contributing something positive to the world.

The constructive question to ask, therefore, is how to encourage companies to get rid of the reasons so many people resent them—while improving their overall contribution to the future. And the good news is . . . that is completely possible to imagine.

The Greed-Only Era Is Waning

For decades, neoliberal economists have argued that free markets can usher in all the progress we need, an argument memorably expressed in the movie *Wall Street,* in which the investment banker Gordon Gekko proclaims, "Greed is good." He was arguing that pure capitalism can make the world better by the productive efficiency of people working in their own self-interest to build things others want and will pay for. He was creepy. But also partly right. Sometimes maximizing profits is in everyone's interest. And any fair historian would confirm that capitalism has played an invaluable role in the world, spreading ideas and wealth.

But that same historian would also have to admit that capitalism can all too easily turn exploitative and damaging. To many millions of people, it seems that we are in that moment right now. Fossil fuels are choking our planet. Big tech is terrifying us. Rising inequality is becoming dangerous. We need to hope for a future where we can somehow replace the greed-only mode of capitalism with something more nuanced, something that takes the public good into account.

Opponents of unfettered capitalism have been fighting this cause for decades, and I see numerous signs that the tide is starting to turn in their favor. They're being helped by the spectacular shift in value over recent decades from the physical to the intangible. Companies used to get rich mainly from physical infrastructure: factories, mines, fleets of trucks, and so on. Today, companies get rich mostly from the creation of intangible assets: software, services, and all manner of knowledge-based work. So they create value not because of machinery or resource extraction, but because of minds. And that means they can't succeed unless they can successfully recruit and motivate those minds.

Guess what? Increasingly, those minds are not willing to work for companies that don't have an inspiring mission and/or won't behave responsibly. Plus, customers and investors are looking for the same values.

Even companies that *do* get most of their value from physical assets are part of this trend, because usually their key to competitive advantage is to leverage the nonmaterial tools of the modern economy, including software, AI, infrastructure engineering, advanced research and development, and effective communications. In other words, they too depend increasingly on the value of talented employees. And they too are subject to the changes in the world at large that are putting greater demands on companies to act for the public good.

One area where this shift has become especially evident in recent years is in the fight against climate catastrophe. The large majority of the world's greenhouse gas emissions is generated by companies, which means that the pathway to a solution will come largely from companies changing what they do. Regulation has a crucial role to play, but there are plenty of signs that the companies themselves *want* to play a positive role.

Goaded by the evident anger and passion of the next generation, corporations have demonstrated a sea change in their attitudes. Many companies today are seriously engaging in efforts to become "net zero" in the near future. Yes, there is much more they can do. Yes, it's critical they continue to push hard in this direction. But I take great heart seeing growing evidence of a commitment to what is probably the single most important form of generosity: generosity to our planet and to our descendants.

The Maersk Story

Take the shipping giant Maersk. Its container ships power global trade—and pump out hundreds of thousands of tons of dirty greenhouse gases each year in the process. But in 2018 its visionary chairman, Jim Hagemann Snabe, and his team set the company on a different path. His board had been debating whether they could actually afford any new measures to reduce emissions. Large ships are much harder to electrify than cars, and all alternatives seemed expensive or unfeasible. But then they realized that they were asking the wrong question. As the market leader, the company had an obligation to find a way to net-zero emissions by 2050. So the right question to ask was, what would it take?

Since no one had an answer, the board decided to invest in a research hub to explore how zero-carbon shipping might possibly be achieved. And they took a further key step, inviting their competitors and suppliers to participate. Three years later, based on the findings of that center, Maersk announced its commitment to new green fuels, created from solar power and offshore wind. Would they be more expensive than today's bunker fuel? Probably. But that needn't stop what had to be done. As Snabe said in his exciting TED Talk, "Even if the green fuel would be two times more expensive than the bunker fuel, it should not be a showstopper. Even at that price, a pair of sneakers, transported from Asia to the US or Europe, would only cost five cents more. The argument around affordability is just a bad excuse for not making the necessary decisions and investments."

This is a form of enlightened corporate generosity. And it is infectious. I've seen plenty of evidence of business leaders encouraging each other to raise their game. If everyone's doing it, it's much easier to tell your shareholders that these are necessary actions to survive and thrive in the twenty-first century.

These actions won't just reduce the threat of climate catastrophe. They will help usher in a future of immense possibility: ultra-low-cost renewable energy, clean air, quiet electric transport, beautiful modern cities with imaginative green spaces, an end to plastic pollution, reforestation, the gradual return of inefficient farmland for nature to rewild.

Commit to generosity, and everyone wins.

And beyond environmental issues, there are many other ways for companies to gain from being generous. Here are two examples.

The Ungreedy Way to Make More Yogurt

The yogurt company Chobani has been famously generous to its employees. At every stage of the company's growth, its founder, Hamdi Ulukaya, focused on recruiting people from struggling rural communities. In 2016, he had two thousand people working for him and donated stock worth an average of $150,000 to each one of them. But these very acts of generosity have helped fuel Chobani's success, both through employee loyalty and the desire of consumers to support brands that stand for something. It has become the leading Greek yogurt brand in the United States, with annual sales of more than $1.4 billion.

In his TED Talk, Ulukaya laid out an "anti-CEO playbook," which has immense power in our connected age: "If you are right with your people, if you are right with your community, if you are right with your product, you will be more profitable, you will be more innovative, you will have more passionate people working for you and a community that supports you. . . . This is the difference between return on investment and return on kindness."

Patagonia's Counterintuitive Rise

For decades, under the leadership of the CEO, Kris Tompkins, and the founder, Yvon Chouinard, the outdoor clothing company Patagonia took actions that seemed to flout its own commercial interests. It decided to pay more for organic cotton to avoid the environmental problems associated with mass-produced cotton. It committed to paying the higher of 1 percent of sales or 10 percent of profits to environmental causes that have helped create vast tracts of wild space in South America. And it implemented generous policies for its employees.

But again, it was these very policies that made the company beloved by so many customers. A survey in late 2022 showed it ranked among the top brands preferred by millennials and Gen Zers, helping generate more than $1 billion in annual sales. And if it wasn't clear that generosity was at Patagonia's core, in 2022 Chouinard donated his economic stake in the company to a trust focused on addressing climate change.

So how can we encourage more companies to embrace this type of thinking?

You Have More Power Than You Know

If you work for a company, you can play your part. A small number of organized employees can shift corporate strategy—your company cannot afford to antagonize its value creators. For example, simply calling a meeting for those interested to discuss your company's po-

tential for being more generous to the planet could build into something unstoppable.

And remember: the Internet can turbocharge every act of generosity, creating the potential for wonderful paybacks. Every company and organization should schedule a daylong retreat once every couple years for some of its most creative thinkers. It should be tasked to answer this single question: What is the most audacious act of generosity we could undertake?

Ideally, this is led from the top, but a small group of employees could also organize this independently. The ideas coming out of it may be just powerful enough to persuade company leadership to act.

Here are some questions to ask in such a brainstorm: Does your company have unique knowledge? It's true that sharing it might reduce your competitive advantage. But it also may give you a global reputation.

Does it have powerful software? What if you opened it up to the world? Yes, you might be giving up a tactical advantage. But independent coders inspired by your open source generosity might help you improve it.

Does it have an archive of valuable photography or music or video? Are you sure there isn't a case to make it freely available to the world? Could that step lead to your being discovered by thousands of people you'd like to know?

Is part of its business model genuinely bad for the planet? Then brainstorm what it would be like to let go of it! Your company's leadership may force competitors to follow suit.

If you spend a day on this, start with all the best brainstorming rules in place. (IDEO has an excellent resource to help here.) Invite people to dream as big as they can. No criticisms allowed until much later. Just invitations to continue to expand the possibility space. Focus on the upsides before you worry about the downsides. And remember that generosity pretty much always evokes a surprising response.

And Now . . . Here Is the News

Imagine, for example, the following headlines coming to your news feed in the next few years.

General Electric launches free courses on wind energy. "We have deep knowledge in how to create superefficient wind turbines. We're going to share that freely with the world so that others can join the race for renewable energy." (Prediction: would help rebuild GE's business through enhanced reputation and new recruits.)

Coca-Cola gives away its secret recipe. "We invite everyone to prepare their own Coke at home. We'll tell you exactly how. And if you can improve the recipe, please let us know. Frankly, we could use an all-natural version with a little less sugar. If your recipe is selected, we'll launch it worldwide, branded as 'the people's Coke,' and pay you $10 million for your contribution." (Prediction: Coke sales increase, and a major new brand is launched.)

Local restaurant offers free Sunday brunch to single parents and their families. "We're all about building community, but some in our community can't afford to go out to eat. So we wanted to do something about that." (Prediction: Goodwill boosts sales enough to make up for the cost. Numerous local businesses are already making offers like this. They're worth cheering on.)

Amazon prioritizes climate over profits. "We're investing $500 million in research on the world's supply chains. As a result, we will be able to place green/amber/red labels on 75 percent of the products we sell according to how climate-friendly they are. On our default search feeds, the green labels will be prioritized." (Prediction: transformative for Amazon's reputation, and allows hundreds of new climate-friendly products to gain market traction.)

What do we get from all this? A future we can get excited about.

And what do the companies themselves gain? Everything. Better employees, passionate customers, a healthier planet, and the restoration of trust and hope.

PHILANTHROPY'S
TRUE POTENTIAL

*What if we gave the world's changemakers
a chance to dream much bigger?*

One of the most important ways we could impact the world is by rethinking how—and how much—we support nonprofits. After all, they are organizations whose very existence depends on generosity. And they are often the most important change agents when it comes to tackling the world's toughest problems.

Are children dying somewhere from starvation or a curable disease? Are people's rights being violated? Is there a societal blind spot that is causing untold misery? Is there an existential danger to humanity's future? In each case, there's a nonprofit somewhere heroically trying to help.

Many of them are run by truly brilliant, dedicated teams. And yet they suffer extreme challenges compared to their counterparts in the for-profit economy, especially when it comes to raising money.

Take a look at this table.

PRIVATELY FUNDED INITIATIVES		
	For-Profit	Nonprofit
>1m lives impacted	MAJOR CORPORATIONS	**?**
<1m lives impacted	SMALL BUSINESSES	ALMOST ALL OF PHILANTHROPY

This shows the landscape of all privately financed projects that make an impact on the world (government initiatives are therefore excluded). The bottom left quadrant covers small businesses—restaurants, local shops, specialty services, and so on. The top left is where much of the economy lives. Corporations with millions of customers, perhaps in multiple countries. When you and I buy a smartphone; drive a car; spend time on Facebook, Netflix, or Google; or buy a share in any Fortune 500 company, we are engaging in that top left quadrant. It drives huge swaths of modern life.

Indeed, whether you look at valuations in the stock market or measure the time you spend with products created by for-profit companies, the majority of the action is in the upper left quadrant. For example, in technology, just eight companies—Apple, Amazon, Microsoft, Google, Nvidia, TSMC, Tesla, and Meta—are worth about as much as all other tech companies combined. Even though a far greater number of companies live in the lower quadrant, their collective impact on us all is materially less than that of the upper quadrant.

Yet when you look at the right half of the landscape, a very different picture emerges. The vast majority of the action is in the *lower* quadrant. In the United States, most philanthropic gifts go to local churches, hospitals, schools, and universities. Their intent is to impact the lives of a few hundred or a few thousand people, not millions. There certainly are major foundations that operate at a larger scale and are doing extraordinary work impacting—in some cases— millions of people. I know many people who have devoted their lives to such efforts and I have huge admiration for what they're doing. But I also feel a sense of outrage on their behalf. Despite the crucial importance of their work, it's rare that they get to dream of projects that would cost, say, $50 million or more. Business operates at a scale that is at least an order of magnitude higher.

Why is this? Is it because somehow nonprofit initiatives can't scale? That it's actually *appropriate* for the majority of philanthropic efforts to be relatively small? No! I believe passionately that we are woefully underestimating what nonprofits could achieve if given a chance.

One of the problems is that the nonprofit world lacks the funding opportunities created by the business world. Let's compare.

A Tale of Two Entrepreneurs

Meet Marcus. He's a passionate young entrepreneur with a proven track record, and now he has a vision for a brilliantly innovative app-based service. It could appeal to people all over the world. He presents his idea to venture capitalists, who back him with three rounds of funding, totaling $25 million (using funds that pool dollars from dozens of early-stage investors). Three years later, he takes his company public, bringing in another $75 million in a single day from thousands of new investors, and two years after that his company is reaching thirty million customers around the world who are delighted with Marcus's Heavenly Pizza app and the drone deliveries that it summons from on high. Marcus is a multimillionaire, and his investors and shareholders have made their mark.

But not everything the world needs can be turned into a profitable product. Three blocks away in the same city lives Maya. She too is a passionate young entrepreneur with a proven track record, and she too has a vision for a brilliantly innovative app-based service that could appeal to people all over the world. In fact, it could transform their lives by offering them crucial help in times of crisis, which is why, inspired by the Carole King song, she names it You've Got a Friend. When people are feeling desperate, they go to the app and find:

- powerful techniques based on proven psychological insights to respond to their pain
- a range of local services they can contact for further help, including counselors available 24/7

But there's a key challenge she has to overcome. Most of the people she's looking to support live in poverty and cannot afford the full cost of her service, which has to be delivered by professionally trained volunteers in every city in which she operates. Governments and employers may eventually pick up the tab, but it will take many years to persuade them to do so. Maya's business plan shows that to have a chance of getting to scale, she'll have to raise $100 million over five years (actually the same amount of capital that Marcus needed).

How does she raise that money? There are no venture capitalists she can approach. There is no equivalent of a public stock market she can tap into. Her best shot at funding her idea is to set up a nonprofit and then approach a range of foundations and individual philanthropists one at a time.

It begins promisingly. Many people express interest in the cause and encourage her to get going and prove that her model is effective. Others offer to fund trials related to specific aspects of poverty and mental health that they have particular reason to care about. After two or three years, she has been able to accumulate a few million dollars and show that her app genuinely helps to break the poverty trap caused by personal crises. But she struggles to find anyone willing to take the risk to blow out the plan aggressively. She spends 50 percent of her time fundraising, and it takes ten meetings on average to get any kind of commitment, which is usually for less than three years and has many restrictions on how she can use the dollars.

Slowly Maya gets burned out. To save her sanity, she decides to cut back her ambitions. Instead of seeking to help people around the world, she finds a funder willing to put in $5 million to subsidize the service for people in her home city. She takes comfort from the fact that over the following years several hundred local people will benefit from her service, which has been diplomatically rebranded to include the name of her donor. Alas, the chance to get to real operational efficiency can't be realized at this scale, and millions of others around the world will suffer their crises alone, never knowing that someone had created the means to lend a hand.

Why do these two stories have such different outcomes? There is no inherent reason why nonprofit initiatives can't generate change at massive scale. They may not be able to self-fund through their own profits, yet there are still multiple ways they can tap into the power of the global economy, the support of the government, or the reach of the Internet. But the reality is that the tools that for-profits have for raising big, multiyear investments just aren't available to them. Nonprofit initiatives are too often funded one donor and one year at a time. It's a deeply inefficient and often frustrating process.

And not just for social entrepreneurs. Private donors—many of whom have gained unprecedented personal wealth in recent years—also dread the endless cycle of fundraising pitches. While they may aspire to do world-changing work through their philanthropy, there's not a ready market for breakthrough ideas that they can tap into. And it can feel risky to go it alone. It's certainly a huge time sink, and they have endless alternative possibilities for how that time is used. So it's no surprise that many with the means and the heart to give big end up sitting on the sidelines.

Thus it is that some of the world's most committed change-makers, both doers and funders, may give up on their biggest dreams. The possibility space of truly audacious change is left underexplored.

What could we do about this?

The key is for both nonprofits and donors to work with each other more creatively, more courageously, more collaboratively. Numerous people are trying to do this in different ways. Let me tell you one such story that I have had an inside view of.

It was inspired by the late Richard Rockefeller, a member of a famously philanthropic family. I had invited him to a meeting of ocean conservationists, and I will never forget the words he spoke: "It's become apparent that many of us here are stressed about the challenges of raising money for these causes we believe in. We find ourselves under extreme pressure to cut back our plans so as to have a chance of getting funded. I think this may be a mistake. In my experience, the wisest and best donors out there are not persuaded by proposals to achieve something small. Here's my suggestion. Ask for more, not less. Be audacious."

Tragically, Richard died in a plane crash four years later. And so he never got a chance to see that his words helped spark a remarkable initiative called . . . yes . . . The Audacious Project.

It brings together a group of visionary foundations led by TED and the Bridgespan Group, an organization devoted to catalyzing bold philanthropy.

Here's how The Audacious Project works:

1. We invite the world's greatest change agents to dream like they've never dreamed before. To create ideas that are truly audacious. Ideas that might impact millions or even hundreds of millions of people, or have environmental impact at planetary scale, or that may be transformative for science or for our long-term prospects of surviving and flourishing. Ideas exciting enough to send a tingle down your spine.

2. We vet the ideas to search for those that genuinely offer a path to execution, scale, and impact. Pick the best of them and help shape them into actionable multiyear plans that are viable and sustainable.

3. We present them to the world in a single moment with as much visibility and excitement as possible and invite people to support

them . . . together. The idea is to use that momentum to build a community of committed supporters around each project who will sustain them over several years, contributing ideas, time, and influence as well as money.

Taken together, our hypothesis was that these three steps could create an exciting marketplace for bold, fundable ideas.

But does this actually work?

Well, we have run this process six times now, presenting a group of bold but carefully vetted ideas to groups of potential donors, and unveiling the successful proposals at TED. The results have been extraordinary. Even in the first year, more than $100 million was committed, far exceeding our expectations. And as we've learned to tweak the process, the amount raised has grown each time. In 2020, despite the challenges of the pandemic, more than $500 million was raised for sixteen different projects. And in early 2023, we broke the $1 billion mark for the first time.

The projects supported include:

- A vision to tackle global hunger by empowering small farmers across the entire continent of Africa to increase their yields by using an effective combination of seeds, training, and financing.
- A major new scientific institution to use the power of CRISPR gene editing to shape the behavior of entire microbiomes with extraordinary potential for both human health and our climate.
- A bold plan to eliminate the terrible eye disease trachoma.
- The launch of a satellite to track emissions of methane, a deadly greenhouse gas.

- Support to enable deworming treatment for one hundred million children who otherwise risk stunted growth.

And here's a surprise. The *process itself* is inspiring, both to the organizations that created the projects and to the individual donors who have the opportunity to work together in service of these big ideas.

All this works only because of the power of infectious generosity. When a group of donors comes together knowing that the groundwork has been laid, it takes just one or two of them to passionately endorse a project to spark a chain reaction. The spark is often as simple as someone saying, "I'm willing to support this if others will join me."

I believe we've only scratched the surface of what's possible. If you have a vision for a better future that could genuinely impact the lives of millions, and a credible plan to realize it, there may well be a way to get it funded at significant scale. In our connected world, we can dream together as never before. And we can come together to make those dreams come true.

Maya, are you listening? This is for you! Instead of hundreds of meetings, you might be able to fund your beautiful idea in a single burst.

Marcus, this might be for you too! Part of the fortune you've made could be reinvested for the public good in ideas that are every bit as bold and entrepreneurial as you are, have been credibly vetted, and will bring you together with other visionary funders.

And as for you, dear reader, this truly is for you as well. This is something we can all participate in. Yes, the scale of funding required for these projects is way out of reach for most individuals. But that's the whole point. This is intended as a means of pooling our efforts. A shared focus on large-scale initiatives is likely to have far more impact than fragmented efforts by siloed individuals.

Scale matters. It brings with it all manner of efficiencies, leverage, brand visibility, and network effects. With scale, you can build a platform, attract partners, and get to critical mass. Even a small contribution to such an effort is likely to achieve more than the same money spent elsewhere. That's because it's helping to accelerate a train that's already moving, helping to make it unstoppable. And it's not just your money that can help. It's your ideas, your encouragement, and your ability to spread the word. All these projects can benefit hugely from a committed community of supporters, cheering them on through thick and thin. Change at scale can't be something that only rich people dream of. It's for all of us.

Your Own Audacious Event?

The success of local giving circles and of The Audacious Project has convinced me that a new model of fundraising could be tried at the local level. Here's how you could team up with a few friends and embark on your own quest to enable an audacious project.

Step 1. Assemble your group of friends and ask this question: Who do we know locally who's trying to solve a problem or work on an exciting project? Or who's done impressive work in the past who may be open to working on something big and new? Try to find at least five individuals or nonprofit groups that could deserve support.

Step 2. Assign one of you to each person or org to do further research. Find out what their funding situation is, what their track record is. Then ask them these questions, which they may never have been asked before: "What's your biggest dream? What could you achieve if the funding was there?" Maybe someone has an idea for a new theater, or a public park, or a soup kitchen, or an imaginative activities center.

Step 3. Meet again with your friends, and winnow down your list to three projects that are both exciting and credible. You need to be persuaded that they truly can be achieved if the funding comes through.

Step 4. Invite the creators of those three projects to turn them into a credible action plan that includes answers to these questions: What is the big idea? Why would it make a huge difference to your neighborhood? How much would it cost? How would that money be spent? (There will need to be a budget with at least the main items covered.) What local hurdles would need to be cleared, e.g., planning? How can we be confident that you would succeed in doing all this?

Step 5. Okay, this may be the hardest part. You need to find a way of reaching out to every potential local donor you can think of. Divide efforts among your group. If everyone has a list of five people to approach, it's a manageable task. Look for local business owners and other successful or influential people in your community. Getting access to them will be hard. But usually you can find a contact point online, perhaps on LinkedIn. And once you've got to one, they should be able to help you reach others. What's in your favor is that you have something really exciting to share with them: Effectively, you're offering them a chance to become a local hero. Tell them this: that you're organizing a local meeting at which three exciting projects will be unveiled that could change your community forever, and that their presence there would mean so much to so many people. Tell them that you want them there for their ideas, not just their money. Tell them there will be no obligation on them to donate. They should do so only if the project excites them. Tell them they'll be part of something that's never been done before, but that has every chance of being amazing. The first big name is the hardest. Once you have that, you can name-drop your way to the rest.

Step 6. Hold the meeting—perhaps in someone's home. People should commit to coming for ninety minutes. You probably want to limit numbers to no more than twenty. Spend the first minute inviting everyone to get ready to think big about the future possibilities in your community, and how beautiful it would be if, by any chance, you could get something funded together. Then give each project lead a maximum of ten minutes to present their idea, encouraging them to focus on two main things: why this would be great for the neighborhood and how it will get done. Follow up each presentation with ten to fifteen minutes of Q and A. Wrap up by inviting donors to sign up for a follow-up meeting with the project or projects they're most excited about. Seeing how many people sign up for each follow-up meeting will tell you a lot. It's possible that one or more of the projects will fail to attract any follow-up support. But hopefully at least one does, and maybe all three.

Step 7. Hold the follow-up meetings separately. At least one of your group should be present at each of them to guide the process. This is when the rubber hits the road. The project lead can dive into their plan in more detail and answer any remaining questions. With twenty minutes left on the clock, ask the project lead to leave the room and then tell the donors: "This is it. This is our chance, while we're all gathered here together. Are some of you willing to go in together to support this project?"

If everyone approaches this with an open mind and a readiness to get excited, don't be surprised to see a generosity infection start spreading before your eyes. There's a chance you raise enough in that moment to completely fund the project. Alternatively, you may get only partway but have enough momentum and excitement to consider how to get the rest of the funding from others in the community.

And even if you fail to raise any money then and there, I'm guessing you'll still have succeeded in sparking some beautiful ideas that may one day see the light of day.

The point is that by going through this process, you're breaking through the silos that stop so many possibilities from ever being realized. We're social animals. We get huge energy from doing things together. When a community comes together and different members can see others' engagement and excitement, everything changes. What seems impossible can become real. In principle, this process could bring rich and poor together in a beautiful way, replacing resentment with excitement and mutual encouragement. It's worth a try.

At infectiousgenerosity.org, we're compiling stories of neighborhoods that have used this approach to get things funded. If you're successful in carrying out this experiment, please tell us! We're learning from each other. And the spirit of audacity is spreading. . . .

The Power of Dreams

The future the world needs will be one in which nonprofit organizations play a far bigger role than they do today. I'm a big believer in the power of the market. But as societies get richer, it makes less and less sense for market forces alone to capture the efforts and dreams of the majority of their citizens. Why should they? When an organization is set free to define its purpose to advance the public good in some way—as opposed to advancing the interests of shareholders—it opens the door to a rich ecosystem of unlimited potential. Instead of just making a product or marketing a service, those organizations can address *any problem* the world faces. Or they can seek to unlock *any opportunity* that human imagination can conjure up.

It's crazy for our collective efforts to be limited to those that can be funded through profits. Audacious generosity could make possible a new generation of nonprofit initiatives that attract the world's most talented people.

The biggest drivers of change should come from the people on the ground actually doing the work. We need to free them from the absurd rigors of fundraising so that they can focus on building a better future. What if we gave them that chance? To dream as big as they can, and then for millions around the world to come together and help turn those dreams into reality.

There's a beautiful virtuous cycle we can collectively unlock here. Greater generosity could enable bolder, more exciting visions for change, which could in turn inspire more generosity. And in our connected world, the ripple effects from these acts can travel far and wide.

What might those bolder visions look like? It's an exciting thing to contemplate.

The incredible agenda set out by Natalie Cargill in the next chapter shows what could ultimately be achieved. But those top-level visions will have to be built up of extraordinary work by thousands of organizations. What could a single organization dream of delivering?

If you're the dreaming kind, try imagining the kind of world-changing initiatives you'd love to see. It's a fun exercise! Here are some examples that came up the last time I tried this:

- A Manhattan Project for the future of the planet. We know how to tackle the climate crisis. We're just not moving fast enough.
- A huge exhibition in a repurposed factory using different art forms to tell untold stories of change-making heroes. It could launch a thousand artists' careers, energize a city, and inspire millions.
- An education bank account for every citizen of the planet, recording every online educational resource they've engaged in, and therefore becoming the ultimate résumé, helping them find their own best journey to employment and empowerment.
- The subsidized provision of solar power direct to the rooftops of every family currently without electricity.
- A world music anthem made up of the voices of millions of people from around the world fused in gorgeous harmony by a combination of musical genius and AI. Once started, it would never cease.
- An online initiative to organize a cleanup of our planet, using thousands of local teams of volunteers, cheered on by a vibrant online community who can't believe the before-and-after photographs.
- A major research institution to investigate what new forms of capitalism and democracy could look like in the modern era.
- A crypto coin to put a price on carbon, backed by a nonprofit that can issue credible contracts for carbon sequestration. Each coin represents the sequestering of one ton of CO_2. High demand for the coin could raise the price of carbon globally and help fund sequestration at scale.
- A future-proof floating city with vibrant life both above and below the ocean's surface.
- A network of underwater webcams maintained in gorgeous lo-

cations to enable free virtual aquariums in every home. The tragedy for ocean life is that it's invisible. It needn't be. This would be a low-cost way to help the world fall in love with it.

- A council of one hundred business leaders, artists, and scientists from the United States and China, seeking to build crucial new bridges between the world's superpowers before they declare war on each other.

- A massive effort to tackle the obesity crisis, bringing together doctors, psychologists, agriculturalists, nutritionists, urban designers, and storytellers.

- A scientific voyage into the depths of the earth. The future of our energy supply and the mystery of life's origins may be found there.

- A large-scale effort at independent content moderation to elevate truth and trust in social media—Wikipedia on steroids (as discussed briefly in chapter 10).

- A space telescope one hundred times more powerful than the already incredible James Webb. (SpaceX's new Starship makes it imaginable.)

- A massive transfer of wealth directly into the newly created bank accounts of the world's poorest.

- A galvanized effort to deepen and accelerate collaboration among the world's scientists to tackle existential threats to humankind.

- A project to collect the best of human culture and achievement from every nation and preserve it in an archive that can survive nuclear war, meteor strike, or climate catastrophe.

- A global passport offering identity, connection, and hope to all who yearn for humanity to move beyond nationalism.

You may think some of these are silly. But tell me. Shouldn't we be having dreams like these, or like your better versions of these? Many of the above ideas could be accomplished handsomely for less than $1 billion. There is enough private philanthropic capital out there to fund one thousand such ideas.

So let's stop kvetching about how annoying philanthropy is and use the power of our collective imaginations to lift it to a whole new level.

THE PLEDGE THAT COULD
CHANGE EVERYTHING

What if we could agree on a single generous
commitment to one another?

When I was fifteen years old, I suffered a crisis of conscience that has stayed with me since. In this chapter, I'm hoping finally to shake it off.

It happened in church. I was sitting, listening to an inspiring visiting speaker. He had devoted his life to working for the world's poor. He spoke about how exhausting the work was, but said that whenever he thought he just had to get some sleep, he remembered the awful hardship being experienced by those he was caring for, and realized that his tiredness was nothing compared to that.

His words filled me with gloom.

I wanted to be a good person. I really did. But it seemed that that meant having to commit to a life of perpetual sacrifice. No matter how hard you were working or what challenges you put yourself through, there would always be others out there somewhere in the world whose suffering demanded that you push yourself that bit harder. Suddenly the future seemed an impossibly tough challenge.

It's not easy to see the way out of this. The philosopher Peter Singer has pointed out that there is no clear moral difference between refusing to help a child dying in front of you and refusing to send financial support to an organization that can save a child on the other side of the world. We no longer live in a world of isolated communities where our obligations extend only to those we're proximate with. Today we can, if we take a moment, see anyone anywhere. And we can do things that have impact anywhere in the world. Therefore, is there any excuse at all not to do so?

Numerous charities out there can credibly claim to save a life in the developing world for less than $5,000. Or to convert a year of suffering into a year of dignity for less than $100. Do you have $100? Which is more important, to buy your next twenty-five cups of coffee or to relieve someone's suffering for a whole year?

But after you've done that once, can you justify stopping? Isn't there a case that you should continue to research and fund such interventions until you yourself are penniless and exhausted? Can you ever sip a latte with a clear conscience again?

Most people's response to these thoughts is to sigh and change the subject. We use canned, unexamined phrases like "Well, there's only so much we can do." Or "It won't do any good to burn out, will it?" Without ever asking whether we ever came close to truly doing *all* that we could do, or whether, honestly, burnout was an imminent danger.

The Traditions That Could Guide Us to a New Norm

How should we address this? Here are some principles we could bear in mind:

1. What if there were an agreed societal norm for giving? This would act as a spur to everyone who wanted to do the right thing while lifting the threat of an unlimited moral burden.
2. The ideal norm should provide enough money to take on the main problems that charitable giving could reasonably tackle.
3. But it should not be so demanding that most human beings, trying to make a go of life in the modern world, would be crushed by it. Moral rules need to seem achievable by the majority of people for them to have credence.
4. It should be accepted as fair, making heavier demands on those who can afford to give more.

So what might such a norm look like? Well, it turns out that this is an issue that has been thought about for many centuries by the world's great religions. All religions seek to offer people a pathway to a joyful, fulfilled life while at the same time laying down moral rules to look after society's neediest.

Two big principles have emerged in different religions. I think it's reasonable to think of them as a pragmatic compromise between the call of conscience and the realities of life. Even though they have been implemented in slightly different ways in different places, broadly speaking, both have survived centuries of practice. Their names are tithing and zakat.

Tithing

In both Judaism and Christianity, there is a long tradition of suggesting that those who are not poor should pay a tithe of 10 percent of their income. In some traditions this was to be paid directly to the church or synagogue, and in others, it was simply a guideline for how much you should contribute to the needy.

Zakat

Meanwhile, in Islam, the principle that emerged focused not on income but on the total wealth that someone owned. Everyone who has wealth above a certain threshold is urged to donate one-fortieth of that wealth (2.5 percent) each year to those in need. This idea, called zakat, is described as Islam's third pillar. It's absolutely core to Islamic religious practice.

The beauty of these traditions is that they bring clarity to the question. These are truly significant amounts to give away. But for many, it's an obligation that is manageable. Once that obligation is met, there is no need for further stress.

Which of these principles is more demanding? Well, it depends how wealthy someone is relative to their annual income. If your total wealth is more than four times greater than your total income, it is harder to meet the demands of zakat. If it's less than four times your income, then it's harder to tithe.

As a very broad rule of thumb, in the modern world, the wealthier someone is, the more likely it is that zakat would be a heavier burden than tithing. A middle-class family in the United States may have a joint income of $90,000 with minimal savings and own a house worth $500,000, offset by a $400,000 mortgage. Their net wealth is about $100,000, barely more than their income. For them, tithing is harder than zakat. Tithing would imply annual giving of $9,000, while zakat would be $2,500.

By contrast, the top 1 percent of Americans have incomes of more than $1 million, and a net worth more than ten times their income. For them, zakat would be much more expensive than tithing.

If you're a religious person and already adhering to one of these commitments, I salute you. It's hard to do. You're being generous. I would definitely encourage you to be sure the money is being spent as strategically as it should for maximum benefit. Some religions seek to sweep up a huge part of their followers' contributions either in alms for the poor, which arguably is not the best way to empower the poor, or in direct contributions to your church, mosque, temple, or synagogue. Perhaps there are better uses of the money. But I salute your willingness to sacrifice your own needs for something outside yourself.

And if (like me) you're not a religious person, I have a question

for you: *Don't we aspire to having ethical standards that at least match or even exceed the religious traditions?*

We live in a world of far greater abundance than that in which those traditions emerged. Yet it's a world facing challenges that could destroy all that we've built. Don't we have a duty to play our fair part in addressing those challenges?

This is something that needs to be a collective effort of all humans.

The Best of Both Worlds

I invite you therefore to consider doing something brave and potentially life-changing: *Embrace both traditions!* Make it your life goal to be able to commit annually the *higher* of 10 percent of your income or 2.5 percent of your net worth.

Now, this is not something you have to do in one leap. Some of you reading this book are in situations where you simply cannot afford to give anything near this much. Perhaps you're early in your career and facing a mountain of student debt. Or you're a struggling single parent navigating the cost-of-living crisis. Or you're out of work. Or you have impossibly high familial obligations. Or you're below the poverty line. No wise moral rules make demands that cannot be met.

Yet what's amazing is that even the poorest in society do still give to others. In fact, they often give a higher percentage of their meager income than those with wealth. Surveys in Western countries typically suggest that people in the poorest income brackets give away 3 to 4 percent of their income, while the wealthiest often give at barely half that level.

So, no matter your circumstance, I do think there's a case to pledge *something*. For most people the income pledge is easier to calculate and to enact. You could start with 3 percent of your income and plan to build it up steadily from there, perhaps adding another percentage point each year that your income rises, until you get to 10 percent. A key benefit of having a pledge is that it will help shift your giving from impulsive to strategic. If you know how much you need to give during a month or during a year, it will really encourage you to spend time thinking of its best use. It also means that we can view our commitments as a collective effort. We're all in this together. We can draw inspiration from the fact that many are doing their fair part.

As I look back at my own history of giving, I'm reminded of just how tough an ask this is. There have definitely been years when, despite significant entrepreneurial success, I haven't given away as much as these pledges would have required. And no doubt I could come up with very good excuses for not doing so, including times when my business crashed in value or I was just too busy to pay attention.

But the more I've thought about generosity, the impact it can have, and the joy it can bring, the more determined I've become to make it an absolute core part of my identity. Jacqueline's work as a pioneering social entrepreneur has inspired me, and together we're now ready to sign that combination pledge, effectively committing to giving the higher of 10 percent of our income or 2.5 percent of our net worth in any given year for the rest of our lives.

The Giving What We Can Pledge

We're making that commitment at the website GivingWhatWeCan .org. Since 2009, Giving What We Can has been encouraging people to make the 10 percent of income pledge. I've been speaking with them about this issue and I'm excited to share that in the run-up to the publication of this book, they have agreed to add the ability to also pledge a percentage of your wealth. This means you could decide to take the same pledge that Jacqueline and I have: to give the greater of 10 percent of our income or 2.5 percent of our wealth. If that's not a realistic starting point for you, they also allow you to customize your pledge so that you can start with a smaller commitment and step up to higher amounts when your circumstances permit. To help you decide what's right for you, they provide interactive tools and advice to help you figure out how much to pledge based on your personal circumstances. Wherever you start, you can easily monitor your pledge over time, and discover a whole community of people around the world who are committed to generosity.

I'd also like to encourage you to invite your friends, family members, work colleagues, religious groups, and giving circles to pledge alongside you. As I think about infectious generosity, this gets me excited. Pledges may be daunting individually, but members of a group can get encouragement and delight from one another. And if we're willing to make our pledges public, as the site encourages, it generates a means for pledging itself to spread.

One key benefit of this expanded pledge is that it can encourage the wealthy to play their full part. For many of the world's richest, income is a fraction of their net worth. For them, 10 percent of income may not be a challenging ask at all. But 2.5 percent of their net worth annually really is. Today, it's estimated that on average the ultra-wealthy give away less than 1 percent of their net worth annually. So this would represent something like a tripling of their giving.

At the very high end, billionaires could, I think, consider stepping up to still higher percentages over time. They have access to wonderful investment opportunities, and for most of them, even after taxes, their wealth is accumulating at a rate well above 5 percent annually. So, unless they can figure out a way to eventually move their giving level well above that annual goal of 5 percent, they will simply be sitting on an ever larger cash pile until they die, representing an extraordinary missed opportunity for them to apply the same skills that made them wealthy to something special for the public good. The new tools from Giving What We Can enable and encourage this process of stepping up to higher-level pledges over time. They can be employed by those struggling to make ends meet *and* by the world's wealthiest.

So the dream here is that rich and poor alike can join forces in a shared mission to move beyond instinctive in-the-moment philanthropy and instead build into our lives a commitment—a commitment to give an amount annually that is customized to our circumstances, but that will nonetheless challenge and inspire us to be generous at a whole new level.

The Incredible World of Maximum Philanthropy

But would all this pledging actually get the job done? Would it raise enough money to effectively address the problems we face? Surely the world has an infinite number of problems and therefore an infinite number of ways for generosity to fall short?

But actually the world *isn't* infinite. And neither are its problems.

Huge, yes. Infinite, no. There is, of course, no absolute way to calculate what it would cost to solve *all* the problems that generosity could solve. But nonetheless some remarkable work has been done to give a sense of what might be possible and what it would cost.

One of the best minds working on this is Natalie Cargill, founder of the strategic giving consultancy Longview Philanthropy. I reached out to her for her best shot at answering this question: What could philanthropy achieve if this combined giving pledge was widely adopted? Now, if literally everyone participated to the max, the pledge would raise more than $10 *trillion* annually, an astounding amount of money. That's about ten times what is currently being given. But we know that many won't be able to afford to participate in full, and others will prefer not to. So for the purposes of this thought experiment, I invited Natalie to lay out what could be done with just one-third of this amount, or about $3.5 trillion per year. Perhaps, just perhaps, we can imagine a world in which we could collectively step up to that.

What she came back with took my breath away. She had taken a long list of the world's greatest challenges, and researched and costed the most promising philanthropic strategies for tackling them at scale.* Her blue-skies plan for $3.5 trillion of annual philanthropy over ten years would do *all* the following:

- End world hunger (today forty-five million children suffer from malnutrition).
- Defeat the "big three" public health killers: tuberculosis, HIV, and malaria.

---

* Of course, there's a difference between a strategy and an actual operational plan. As anyone who's worked to change any kind of system knows, even with money behind you, it's extraordinarily difficult to be effective. The purpose here is simply to show the scale of what we could legitimately dream of achieving.

- Free everyone who is a modern-day slave.
- Cover the costs of resettling all the 6.6 million refugees who live in refugee camps.
- Ensure universal access to basic water supply and adequate sanitation.
- Provide universal access to affordable and clean energy in the developing world.
- Provide high-quality, universal education at the pre-primary, primary, and secondary levels.
- End neglected tropical diseases, such as Chagas disease, Guinea worm disease, and leprosy.
- Improve maternal and child health in developing countries, saving the lives of nineteen million mothers and two million children and newborns each year.
- Save or plant a trillion trees by 2050 through forest restoration and protection.
- Increase the amount of solar energy produced per year by ten times.
- Build a system of wastewater monitoring and rapid diagnostics to detect every potential pandemic before it begins.
- Develop the production capacity to produce vaccines for everyone in the world in three months if a new pandemic breaks out.
- Stockpile enough "pandemic-proof PPE" for every essential worker to ensure society can operate even under the most extreme pandemics.
- Install germicidal light to cleanse the air of 90 percent of viruses and bacteria in every hospital and the top one hundred international airports worldwide.
- Support a safe and beneficial transition to general artificial in-

telligence by growing the fledgling field of AI safety to 10 percent of global AI investments.

- Make meat alternatives as cheap and tasty as the real thing.
- Give meat alternatives the same advertising budget as the meat industry.
- Prevent the 1.5 million annual deaths from indoor air pollution.
- Prevent three million heart attacks in the developing world.
- Work with organizations like GiveDirectly to eliminate extreme poverty by providing a universal basic income for the entire world.

(You can find a link to Natalie's full incredible worksheet at infectiousgenerosity.org.)

Of course, accomplishing all these tasks would require an effort unlike anything the world has ever seen. It would need political buy-in from recipient countries and the active participation and expansion of pretty much every nonprofit that has ever worked in these areas. But those are steps that in themselves will create jobs and boost our long-term capacity for making change. And Natalie was quick to point out that these are not even necessarily the most cost-effective interventions, just those where there are specific proposals out there on how to implement and scale.

All this may sound crazy to you. After all, efforts at change at massive scale can easily run into unexpected problems and unintended consequences. For example, years of financial aid by the world's governments have often had disappointing or even negative results.

Nonetheless, each of the outcomes listed above has detailed financial estimates behind it, and we're opening up all of them to invite discussion on how they could be improved. It's hard to imagine a more significant debate. The end goal is to show what a future lit up by maximum philanthropy could look like. We need that vision to pull us forward. And you have to say that, for a starting lineup, it's a pretty alluring vision.

Maximum philanthropy? Well, yes. It is hard to imagine a scenario where it would make sense to try to raise *more* than that philanthropically. Because at this level, the bottleneck to making change would not be financial. It would be assembling the teams, aligning with governments and companies, and coordinating the other actions needed to achieve the above. If we accomplished all this, no doubt there would be some future in which a wealthy world could spend even more trillions of philanthropy on human flourishing and resilience. But first things first. For now, that list stands as a glittering message of wonder and possibility. An invitation to all of us to dream bigger about what humanity might be capable of.

The Letter I Wish I Could Write

Ever since that day in church half a century ago, I have felt a level of guilt for not doing enough. And a lot of confusion about how even to think of resolving the issue. At last I can feel those clouds lifting. If I could, I would slip a little note inside a time capsule and whisk it back to the younger version of me. This is what it would say:

Dear Fifteen-Year-Old Self,

I have good news. It's going to be okay.

Yes, you do indeed have an ethical obligation to others wherever they are in the world. You should take it seriously. But it is not an impossible burden to carry.

Much of your generosity can be expressed through nonfinancial means. And as far as money goes, the most you need to commit is 10 percent of your income or—if you get really wealthy—2.5 percent of your net worth each year. You can probably handle that. It'll be tough, but worth it.

You'll discover that a commitment to generosity can be your pathway not to guilt but to joy.

You've got this!

With love,
Your lucky, grateful future self

The Wrap

So when you put all these pieces together, something genuinely exciting emerges.

It becomes clear that the two ancient traditions of giving—tithing and zakat—could provide the basis for all the philanthropy the world needs. Spent wisely, this would be more than enough to create the leverage required for a world in which everyone can lead a dignified life, with their basic material needs met. It could also dramatically reduce the risk of existential events threatening our world *and* open the door to countless other possibilities of scientific and artistic discovery.

I find this remarkable. The pledges created by our religious traditions promote a standard of giving that can still work beautifully in our modern era. These are manageable sacrifices for many people, yet they can raise enough money to utterly change our future prospects. Throughout history, most human lives have been spent in extreme poverty, grinding out a way to survive. Today, civilization has generated enough wealth for something entirely different. If we're willing, collectively, to make an affordable sacrifice, we can fund pretty much everything the future needs of us.

In summary: If good-thinking people could agree on a generosity pledge as a social norm, it would do four key things:

- It would give every pledger extra motivation to keep giving, even in years that are tougher, or in which they may otherwise simply forget.
- The concept of the pledge can be easily shared with others, making it its own form of infectious generosity.
- Once the amount pledged is set, pledgers are much more likely to spend time thinking strategically about the best use of their philanthropy, rather than simply responding to one-off appeals.
- And the thrilling big-picture vision of what a fully adhered-to pledge could deliver for the world can unite and inspire people across divisions of nationality, religion, and income.

So I invite you to head over to GivingWhatWeCan.org to take the pledge, and to encourage others to do the same. You can start small and build up to the desired goals of 10 percent of income or 2.5 percent of net worth at whatever pace you can manage. If enough of us do this, it really could change everything.

OVER TO YOU

Invitation to an annual checkup

We've spent part 3 of the book imagining a future in which generosity plays a more prominent role in the world—in the Internet, in business, and in philanthropy.

But how about you? Is there a future in which generosity becomes a richer, deeper, more meaningful part of your life? We've just spent a chapter pondering what a personal financial pledge could look like. But as we've seen, generosity is about far more than giving money. It's about our time, talent, and resources. It's about our very mindset.

What might we do to embrace generosity as a core part of who we are? And how could we measure that? At the outset, we must acknowledge that everyone's situation is different. The astonishing generosity shown every day by a parent looking after a severely disabled child is hard to compare with the generosity of the successful executive who for the most part expresses it financially.

But even with the vast differences in our personal situations, I believe there is a way to pull everyone together in a single, simple, but highly useful framework. It goes back to what I suggested in the introduction could be the single most important question someone might ask of themselves: Am I a net giver or a net taker?

Here's what I propose: Once a year, perhaps as part of our New Year's resolutions, or over a coffee during an annual vacation, or on GivingTuesday in late November, we each commit to spending an hour taking stock of our lives in pursuit of our own answer to this fundamental question.

Of course, there is no clear-cut mathematical way of determining an answer. It's a matter of personal honest reflection. But I've found it helpful to break the question down into seven main parts. You don't need positive answers in every case, but if you can get confident yeses on some of them, then you are on your way.

Here are the seven parts:

1. *Is the work I am doing fundamentally contributing to the world versus exploiting the world?* If you're working for a company or organization whose mission is clearly positive for the public good, that's a huge plus mark in your net-give versus net-take balance sheet. Given how much time we spend at work, it really matters that what we do there is net positive. If it isn't, can you do anything to change that? You may have more power than you know. And if you're not working for someone else, is your own productive time contributing to the public good in some way? If you're a creative who's bringing joy to others or a full-time parent seeking to raise kids you can be proud of, then you're entitled to a positive answer here.

2. *In my personal time, am I regularly acting on behalf of others?* If you're spending more than two hours a week volunteering, acting as someone's caregiver, or advocating on behalf of a cause you believe in, you're being generous with your time. Many people only have about twenty hours of discretionary time a week—time when they're not working, eating, sleeping, or attending to obligations—and allocating 10 percent of this for nonselfish purposes amounts to the time equivalent of tithing. If you clearly have less than twenty hours of discretionary time available to you, it's reasonable to apply the same 10 percent principle to whatever time you do have.

3. *Is my carbon footprint fully offset?* You can use a site like carbonfootprint.com to calculate this. Rather than feel guilty about the results, you could decide to offset it, or—better yet—double-offset it, namely, by buying carbon offsets from a reputa-

ble source equal to twice your estimated annual footprint. This allows a big buffer for the inevitable uncertainty as to your actual footprint and how well the offsets work, and can help you be confident that net-net you're being generous to the planet. For a person with an average lifestyle in the West, a double-offset would cost about $500 a year. Any money spent on carbon offsets can be considered part of your financial giving.

4. *Am I making my personal resources and skills available to others?* Every year, look back to those moments when you've willingly shared something with someone else, whether it's hospitality, a valued possession, knowledge, skills you've been happy to pass on, or opening up your network. Those are all beautiful examples of generosity you can be proud of. Not everyone has the same resources. Among a group of friends, someone may have a house, a double income, and ample childcare, while others are struggling. The question is not whether you are giving as much as others you know; it's whether you are giving more than you're taking.

5. *Am I being generous with my money?* The simplest way to answer this, as recommended in the previous chapter, is to go to GivingWhatWeCan.org, fill in the confidential questions about your financial circumstances, and see how their recommendation compares to what you're actually giving. Your long-term goal is to get to the higher of 10 percent of your income or 2.5 percent of your net worth annually. But many will need time to build up to that level.

6. *Am I practicing a generosity mindset?* This, of course, is the key to all other forms of generosity. Whether you're heading out onto the street, or onto the Internet, it makes all the difference if you're

carrying generosity with you, looking for the best in others and for opportunities to make someone else's day.

A friend of mine who saw an early version of the manuscript that became this book wrote to me something I found deeply moving: "Since I read your draft, I have found myself asking a recurring question: *What is the most generous version of everything I do?* I have asked this within my morning routine; breakfasting healthier to look after myself better, asking my wife what the day ahead of her looks like and how I can help, making sure the hour before my kids' nursery drop-off is full of joy and music and silliness on top of getting them ready. I've asked myself this at coffee shops, supermarkets, car parks; opening doors, engaging in more conversations with strangers, and buying the odd coffee forward. I have asked myself this in regard to the people I know, prompting me to buy gifts for colleagues, and to open our home to a friend going through a divorce. And, of course, I've asked this a million times in my work online."

My friend's beautiful question is born from a generosity mindset and immediately helps amplify that mindset. In the spirit of infectious generosity, I'm going to start asking it of myself, too, and I invite you to do the same. I suspect we won't be able to hold ourselves to that standard all day every day. But if we can find a way to return to it, everything else changes.

And finally . . .

7. *Am I looking for every opportunity for my generosity—and that of others—to become infectious?* This may be the most important question of all. This book is devoted to the idea that we can col-

lectively build a hopeful future if we give generosity its best shot. That means taking every opportunity to notice it and celebrate it, wherever we see it. Look out for the hidden heroes who are toiling away unseen and help make them visible. Use your social media and your social connections to pass on stories that illuminate our better angels. Team up with others and figure out what you can do together that would go beyond your individual efforts. (You can start by just inviting a group of friends to dinner!) Be willing, if the moment is right, to share your own acts of kindness. Generosity *wants* to spread. Let's grant it its wish.

You might think that committing to ask yourself these questions once a year will be daunting and will cause you stress and guilt. I think it will do the opposite. I think this is an invitation to self-knowledge and to decision-making that is profoundly in both your long-term interest and the long-term interest of those you love. It's an invitation to be the person you want to be. It's an invitation to joy.

And if this self-reflection ever leads you to do something kind that you might not otherwise have done, all bets are off. In a time when everyone's connected, a single generous act can have unlimited consequences. I have a final story that illustrates exactly that— somehow the gift of a single box of tissues sparked a movement that inspired hundreds of thousands of people. Here's what happened.

A Kindness Pandemic

In March 2020, Australia went into lockdown. Stories of death, chaos, and grocery hoarding filled the media. The anti-ageism campaigner Catherine Barrett knew that there were stories not being told. Everyone felt on the edge of tears, but lots of people were trying to do something about it. One day, one of her neighbors put a box of tissues on the communal table in her building with just a simple note: Please take if needed. Catherine was deeply touched by the act, because it showed someone acknowledging that everyone was hurting.

And then she had an idea. She created a new group on Facebook called the Kindness Pandemic, and posted a picture of the box of tissues and the neighbor's note. She wrote: "Such a simple gesture that means such a lot. I'm setting this group up to spread Kindness . . . and I also hope the group helps to restore our faith in each other." She invited people to practice "Loud Kindness," sharing their stories and those of others.

The Facebook group grew so quickly that it crashed. "People were tired of the division, tired of the hatred, they were tired of the lack of compassion," remarked Catherine in an interview with Kate. "Across all of the comments, people were saying, 'This is what we need.'" The group quickly grew to more than five hundred thousand people, with members from all over the world telling stories of kind acts they had witnessed or done themselves, week after week. Determined to spread the Kindness Pandemic still further, Catherine did something audacious. She created a simple framework to allow others to take on the Kindness Pandemic brand for themselves so that local groups could be established and coordinate with each other. Before long, more than seventy local Kindness Pandemic Facebook groups were not only spreading stories of kindness but also directing members to local services and resources. And for visitors to all the Kindness Pandemic pages, a heartwarming mosaic emerged of thousands of local and global random acts of kindness. Here are just a few:

Tracey Rohweder: "To the kind lady on the 120 bus yesterday who could see my daughter was upset after she left her bag at the bus stop. Thank you for being the caring, nonjudgmental mum voice she needed. You checked in on her, got her to take some deep breaths. Even offered to ring someone for her. She has anxiety and is on the autism spectrum, so she was frozen with fear. Your kindness got her to uni, and she was able to call me and let me know what happened. And today we got her bag back! You saved the day for her. And me!"

Ginger Rogers: "These flowers were given to me today by a young boy as I walked past his house. He was playing in the garden, saw me, asked me to wait, picked these for me, and put them in my hand. A completely random act of kindness that meant more to me than that little boy could ever know."

Group Member: "My dad's funeral was held today, in Wales, almost 17,000 kms away. I could not be there. The vicar encouraged the family to get my words for my dad recorded and played them in my voice during the ceremony. . . . A complete stranger, Katie, a young woman I have never met, streamed every moment of the funeral to me live, from leaving home, the service, the eulogies . . . walking behind the coffin to the cemetery and burial in a rural Welsh village, so that I could be there, all the way from Australia. And my workmates gift-packaged a soft blanket and care package to support me through a near-midnight live stream. I cannot express how much all these kindnesses are helping me through my grief."

Such stories are continuing to pour in more than two years after the group was founded. It is indeed a kindness pandemic. And it was triggered by a single person doing something that came naturally.

How many more kindness pandemics might there be? In an era when every human is connected to every other human, there truly is no limit. By becoming a net giver, we don't just alter our own lives' balance sheets, we inspire others to be generous too.

We humans need not sleepwalk through our lives. Unlike any other species, we have the ability to step back, reflect, imagine, and make determined decisions, individually and collectively. We're all co-authors of the future. And the story we write together may yet surprise us.

EPILOGUE

So, dear reader, we've been on quite the journey together in search of a new understanding of generosity. You've generously engaged with me in both thought and emotion. But what now? What will you do with all of this? As you return to your busy life, here are the final words I hope you will carry with you. They are a summary, a manifesto, and a love letter.

Every human has the potential to give. The urge to do this is built deep inside each of us, and can be stirred just by our being open to the needs of others. When we share our time, our money, or our creativity, those acts can spark responses in kind. So, once it gets started, generosity can spread like wildfire. As it passes from one person to the next, many lives can be touched. And our collective witnessing of what humans are ca-

pable of can overcome today's prevailing cynicism, bringing people together in common cause.

The Internet offers the possibility of a transformational amplification of human kindness. Until now, it has too often played on our worst instincts, generating outrage, fear, and division. But we can do something about that. Our connectedness allows us to express generosity in ways that were simply impossible before, sharing our best knowledge and creations with potentially millions of people all over the world. And, more than that, it allows us to share stories of generosity in ways that can inspire and delight.

Everyone can play a part here. You don't have to be rich or a creative genius. If you can adopt a generous mindset, seek to understand people you disagree with, and write words that are kind instead of cruel, you can help turn the tide. There's no single pathway to a generous life. But everyone can aspire to give more than they take.

Companies and organizations have a key role to play too. Our connectedness has changed the rules around what we should give and what we should hold on to. Every organization should take a day to dream about what it may give away that could surprise and delight the world. The bolder and more creative you are, the more likely it is that your generosity will create exciting ripple effects that can transform your reputation.

Generosity starts with gratitude. When we pause for a moment, we can remember countless things we can be grateful for. If we make that a beautiful daily habit, it leads naturally to a desire to give back to the universe, to build generosity into our daily lives. This could be as simple as committing to one simple act of kindness every single day or devoting time to a cause we care about by volunteering, mentoring, or engaging in online advocacy. It could also mean taking a financial pledge—donating annually the higher of 10 percent of our income or 2.5 percent of our individual net worth to the causes we have thoughtfully prioritized. If that pledge were widely adopted, it would raise enough money to tackle every single problem that humanity faces.

Even for the most generous among us, it can be hard to know when and how best to give. This is a task for both heart and head. Commit to spending time immersed in an issue you care about. And at the same time ask the big questions: How big is this? How solvable is this? How neglected is this? Look for organizations that are having an impact. Give them a chance with your money. You'll never have certainty around what the "best" use of your money is. It's better to be out there contributing and learning than timidly refusing to take any risks. Most important of all, look for like-minded collaborators. The work of change is a lot more satisfying as a team sport. When we join forces, we can achieve so much more, while also getting more joy from it.

This is a moment to reimagine how generosity could transform us. It's a chance to dream about audacious philanthropy focused on the needs of the whole world. About companies with the vision to get on the right side of history. About a global uprising of ordinary citizens determined to reclaim the Internet and make it a force for good in our world. Are we ready to get excited about the future once again? It's time!

And for you personally, this is all about that most elusive, inspiring, and beautiful thing: the quest for meaning. We were born to be connected. So give in any way that you feel able. Give creatively. Give courageously. Give collaboratively. And let the magic of generosity ripple out into the universe.

If you do that, don't be surprised if one day you wake up and hear a whisper from inside: "I have never felt so happy."

INVITATION

I'd like to invite you to continue your generosity journey at infectiousgenerosity.org.

You'll find more stories there and links to many of the resources referred to in this book.

And you'll get a chance to meet a remarkable AI assistant that we've been creating: Iggy, your partner in kind.

Iggy's purpose is to offer you personalized advice and companionship as you contemplate how you might best contribute. We predict Iggy will, if nothing else, bring a smile to your face.

You'll also find instructions there on how you might easily give copies of *Infectious Generosity* to your friends and colleagues so that you can bring others with you on this journey.

Most important of all, you'll be able to share your own insights and your own stories of infectious generosity. We're eager to hear from you!

ACKNOWLEDGMENTS

This book has been co-created by a host of talented, generous souls.

Kate Honey spent months researching dozens of stories of infectious generosity, turning a dry concept into a hopeful reality. Kate is brilliant, wise, and kind, and has contributed to the book in numerous ways.

Tom Cledwyn is amplifying the book by creating an AI-powered website (infectiousgenerosity.org) and being the mastermind behind our branding and marketing. I'm stunned by his rare combination of deep insight and creative genius.

Our wonderful illustrator, Liana Finck, has brought us all gifts of poignancy, insight, and delight.

Trusted friends and loved ones encouraged me to get started on this project, read early drafts, and saved me from countless missteps and dead ends. Jeanie Honey, Beth Novogratz, Sunny Bates, Chee

Pearlman, Cyndi Stivers, Steve Petranek, Otho Kerr, Arch Meredith, and Rob Reid, I am lucky to know you.

Many TED speakers and other members of the TED community generously gave their time to review and advise, including Jonathan Haidt, Andrew Solomon, Brené Brown, Dan Pallotta, Steven Pinker, Adam Grant, Eli Pariser, David Bodanis, Peter Singer, Scott Cook, Terry Moore, Alain de Botton, Liv Boeree, William MacAskill, Natalie Cargill, and Tom Tierney.

Elizabeth Dunn led the team behind the Mystery Experiment and thereby helped catalyze this book's existence. Other key members of that team included Sheila Orfano, Ryan Dwyer, and Malanna Wheat.

None of this would have been possible without the unique cast of characters who made TED what it is today. A special shout-out to Jay Herratti, Lindsay Levin, Anna Verghese, Helen Walters, Logan Smalley, and Michelle Quint, who all offered invaluable editorial advice and encouragement; and to former colleagues June Cohen and Jason Wishnow, who played a key role in the original release of TED Talks online. But really, to everyone at TED, thank you. You amaze and delight me every day.

An extraordinary team of professionals has gone above and beyond in helping bring this project into the world. Todd Shuster, my agent, has been unwavering in his belief in this book, even when it was just an ill-formed jumble. My editors on opposite sides of the Atlantic, Drummond Moir and Paul Whitlatch, initially crushed me with their honest criticisms of parts of the book, but then showed me how to recraft it into something workable. They are so talented and clearheaded. Indeed, the whole team at Penguin Random House, masterminded by visionary publisher David Drake, has been off-the-charts great: creative, bold, diligent, and—yes—generous.

My mother, Gwendy Anderson, has spent the last two decades in a nursing home, her beautiful mind destroyed by a stroke. I'll never be able to tell her this now, but her determined insistence on never judging someone without truly knowing their story is the reason I placed "generosity mindset" at the heart of this book.

Zoe Anderson embodied generosity in its sparkliest, most glorious form. Her life was cut tragically short at twenty-four years, but her spirit lives on in all who knew her, the most beautiful, poignant example of infectious generosity that I know of.

I am so lucky to have a family that brings me joy and gratitude every single day: my amazing daughters, Elizabeth and Anna; sons-in-law, Joe and Sam; grandkids, Zander, Clara, and Maeva; and my life partner, Jacqueline, who lives a life of generosity, love, determination, and courage at a level I can only marvel at.

My final acknowledgment is to all those unsung heroes who have devoted time, talent, and money to something beyond themselves. There are literally billions of you out there. And you are shapeshifting the future toward hope.

RESOURCES

All of the following, and more, can be linked to easily from infectiousgenerosity.org.

Recommended Books

Bregman, Rutger. *Humankind: A Hopeful History.* London: Bloomsbury, 2019.

Coombes, Joshua. *Do Something for Nothing: Seeing Beneath the Surface of Homelessness, Through the Simple Act of a Haircut.* London: Murdoch Books, 2021.

Dickson, Mike. *Our Generous Gene.* Generous Press, 2016.

Dunn, Elizabeth, and Michael Norton. *Happy Money: The New Science of Smarter Spending.* London: Oneworld Publications, 2014.

Guzmán, Mónica. *I Never Thought of It That Way: How to Have Fearlessly Curious Conversations in Dangerously Divided Times.* New York: BenBella Books, 2022.

Hopkins, Rob. *From What Is to What If: Unleashing the Power of Imagination to Create the Future We Want.* London: Chelsea Green Publishing, 2019.

MacAskill, William. *What We Owe the Future: A Million-Year View.* London: Oneworld Publications, 2023.

Ryan, M. J. *Radical Generosity: Unlock the Transformative Power of Giving.* Newburyport, MA: Conari Press, 2018.

Singer, Peter. *The Life You Can Save: How to Play Your Part in Ending World Poverty.* Basingstoke, UK: Picador, 2010.

Smith, Christian, and Hilary Davidson. *The Paradox of Generosity: Giving We Receive, Grasping We Lose.* Oxford, UK: Oxford University Press, 2014.

Wahba, Orly. *Kindness Boomerang: How to Save the World (and Yourself) Through 365 Daily Acts.* New York: Flatiron, 2017.

Williams, Matthew. *The Science of Hate.* London: Faber and Faber, 2021.

TED Talks

Available via Ted.com or YouTube.

Mike Dickson: "What is enough?"

Elizabeth Dunn: "Helping others makes us happier—but it matters how we do it."

Michael Norton: "How to buy happiness."

Mary Portas: "Welcome to the Kindness Economy."

Alex Sandler: "What is a gift economy?"

Orly Wahba: "Making kindness viral."

Adam Grant: "Are you a giver or a taker?"

Melinda and Bill Gates: "Why giving away our wealth has been the most satisfying thing we've done."

Dan Harris: "The benefits of not being a jerk to yourself."

Sara Lomelin: "Your invitation to disrupt philanthropy."

Mundano: "Trash cart superheroes."

Daniel Pallotta: "The way we think about charity is dead wrong."

Peter Singer: "The why and how of effective altruism."

John Sweeney: "Why kindness matters."

Alain de Botton: "Atheism 2.0."

Nicholas Christakis: "The hidden influence of social networks."

Lily Yeh: "From broken to whole."

Jon Ronson: "When online shaming goes too far."

Jim Hagemann Snabe: "Dreams and details for a decarbonized future."

Daryl Davis: "Why I, as a black man, attend KKK rallies."

Dylan Marron: "Empathy is not endorsement."

Hamdi Ulukaya: "The anti-CEO playbook."

Sir Ken Robinson: "Do schools kill creativity?"

Jeffrey Walker: "Creating whole-table discussions over dinner."

Priya Parker: "3 steps to turn everyday get-togethers into transformative gatherings."

Podcasts

Chesterfield, Alex, Laura Osbourne, and Ali Goldsworthy. *Changed My Mind.* Depolarisation Project.

GoodGoodGood. *Sounds Good with Branden Harvey.*

Karabell, Zachary, and Emma Varvaloucas. *What Could Go Right?* The Progress Network.

Marron, Dylan. *Conversations with People Who Hate Me.*

Voss, Michael Gordon. *Giving with Impact.* The episode "Giving Circles for Greater Community Impact" is particularly recommended.

Philanthropy and Generous Living

Giving What We Can is a research body advising donors on the most effective charities: www.givingwhatwecan.org.

GiveWell researches outstanding giving opportunities for donors to make maximum impact: www.givewell.org.

The Audacious Project identifies bold but credible ideas for collaborative support: www.audaciousproject.org.

GivingTuesday is a nonprofit and global movement that has inspired hundreds of millions to be generous on the Tuesday following Thanksgiving: www.givingtuesday.org.

GiveDirectly is a nonprofit that allows donors to transfer money directly to the world's poorest households: www.givedirectly.org.

Acumen is a global community financing businesses with "patient capital," lifting millions out of poverty in the developing world: https://acumen .org.

Life Vest Inside, founded by TED speaker Orly Wahba, is a nonprofit organization "dedicated to inspiring, empowering, and educating people of all backgrounds to lead a life of kindness": www.lifevestinside.com.

The website What Is a Giving Circle? (created by Philanthropy Together) is an entertaining and informative how-to guide for starting a giving circle, and why you should: https://whatisagivingcircle.com.

Grapevine.org is an organization that provides free digital infrastructure for groups of friends to set up their own giving circle: www.grapevine.org.

Every.org is an organization offering digital fundraising infrastructure for charities of all sizes: www.every.org.

Solutions-Based Journalism

Future Crunch is a hub of positive global trends grounded in data, with an
inspiring weekly newsletter of stories for subscribers: https://
futurecrunch.com.

Reasons to Be Cheerful was founded by the musician David Byrne, and the
website collates "smart, proven, replicable solutions to the world's
most pressing problems": https://reasonstobecheerful.world.

Positive News is a cooperatively owned print and online magazine "joining
the dots between how people, communities, and organizations are
changing the world for the better": www.positive.news.

GOOD Worldwide is a B-corp social-impact company focused on human
progress, with an audience of 150 million people. It has two main
media branches: Upworthy delivers feel-good inspiration, whereas
GOOD features in-depth analysis and reporting: https://goodinc.com.

Bridging and Hospitality

Bridging organization Living Room Conversations has published one hundred free conversation guides to help bring people together on conten-
tious issues: https://livingroomconversations.org/topics/.

Bridging organization Braver Angels offers a free e-course on how to respectfully connect online: https://braverangels.org/online-skills-for
-social-media/.

The Big Lunch is an annual, global neighborhood get-together, generating
new connections, celebrating community, and helping people make
change where they live: www.edenproject.com/mission/our-projects/
the-big-lunch.

StoryCorps is an organization devoted to sharing people's stories "in order
to build connections . . . and create a more just and compassionate
world": https://storycorps.org.

We Are Weavers, founded by TED speaker David Brooks, supports a philosophy of "deep relationships and community success" over individual achievement: https://weareweavers.org.

BridgeUSA's "Let's F***ing Talk to Each Other" campaign focuses on
combating polarization on college campuses and beyond: www
.bridgeusa.org/lets-f-ing-talk/.

NOTES

Introduction

xvi **The greater the sense:** Jim Davies, "We Aren't Selfish After All," *Nautilus,* April 29, 2020, https://nautil.us/we-arent-selfish-after-all -237799.

xvi **When the clip was posted online:** Reddit user T6900, "R/humans beingbros—Random downpour in DC, this guy jumps out of his car to share an umbrella with a couple down on their luck." Reddit, 2022, www.reddit.com/r/HumansBeingBros/comments/u57grb/random _downpour_in_dc_this_guy_jumps_out_of_his/.

Chapter 1: Inside a Contagion

6 **TED Talks have been translated:** "TED Translators," TED, 2023, www.ted.com/about/programs-initiatives/ted-translators.

8 *Harvard Business Review:* Nilofer Merchant, "When TED Lost Control of Its Crowd," *Harvard Business Review,* April 2013, https:// hbr.org/2013/04/when-ted-lost-control-of-its-crowd.

10 **As of 2023:** Data from www.joshtalks.com/josh-talks/.

11 **"The only way we'll do it":** Ken Robinson, "Do schools kill creativ-

ity?,'" TED, 2006, www.ted.com/talks/sir_ken_robinson_do_schools
_kill_creativity.

Chapter 2: The Infinite Village

16 **Wildlife sound recordist:** Andy Corbley, "Wildlife Sound Recordist
Releases Treasured Audio Collection for Free—to Awe and Inspire
the World," Good News Network, February 23, 2022, www.good
newsnetwork.org/200-of-martyn-stewart-sound-records-are-available
-for-free-on-soundcloud.

17 **Bridging organization Living Room Conversations:** "Conversation
Topics," Living Room Conversations, 2023, https://livingroom
conversations.org/topics/.

17 **US hip-hop duo Run the Jewels:** Daniel Kreps, "Run the Jewels to
Make New Album 'Free for Anyone Who Wants Some Music,'" *Rolling Stone,* May 31, 2020, www.rollingstone.com/music/music-news/
run-the-jewels-4-free-1008096.

17 **The iconic French photographer:** Yann Arthus-Bertrand, "A wide-
angle view of fragile earth," TED, 2009, www.ted.com/talks/yann
_arthus_bertrand_a_wide_angle_view_of_fragile_earth.

17 **YouTuber @joejoezidane:** YouTube account @HUMAN The movie,
"HUMAN The movie (Director's cut version)," YouTube, April 14,
2020, www.youtube.com/watch?v=fC5qucSk18w.

18 **Likewise, the ability for musicians:** Clare Mulroy, "Spotify Pays Artists (Sort of), but Not per Stream. Here's How It Breaks Down," *USA
Today,* October 22, 2022, https://eu.usatoday.com/story/life/2022/
10/22/how-much-per-spotify-stream/8094437001.

19 **"I've got to build something":** Interview of Matthew Burrows by
Kate Honey, May 5, 2022.

21 **To take the example of Patreon:** "Our Story," Patreon, 2023, www
.patreon.com/about.

23 **When billionaire Robert Smith:** Dimitra Kessenides, "Robert Smith
Pays Off Student Loans at Morehouse College," *Bloomberg News,*
December 14, 2019, www.bloomberg.com/news/articles/2019-12
-04/robert-smith-pays-off-student-loans-at-morehouse-college.

24 **Back in 2014:** Jon Ronson, "When online shaming goes too far,"
TED, July 20, 2015, www.ted.com/talks/jon_ronson_when_online
_shaming_goes_too_far.

25 **The philosopher Alain de Botton:** Alain de Botton, "Atheism 2.0,"
TED, 2011, www.ted.com/talks/alain_de_botton_atheism_2_0.

Chapter 3: Imperfect Generosity

32 **For what it's worth:** Wayne E. Baker and Nathaniel Bulkley, "Paying It Forward vs. Rewarding Reputation: Mechanisms of Generalized Reciprocity," *Organization Science* 25, no. 5 (Oct. 2014): 1493–510, https://doi.org/10.1287/orsc.2014.0920.

33 **The fact that CEOs:** Kate Gibson, "It Takes 300 Worker Salaries to Equal the Average CEO's Pay, Data Show," CBS News, July 14, 2021, www.cbsnews.com/news/ceo-pay-300-worker-salaries-compensation.

33 **And it is shocking:** Credit Suisse Research Institute, *Global Wealth Databook 2022,* Credit Suisse, 2022, www.credit-suisse.com/media/assets/corporate/docs/about-us/research/publications/global-wealth-databook-2022.pdf.

34 **As the French economist:** Thomas Piketty, *Capital in the Twenty-First Century* (Cambridge, MA: Harvard University Press, 2014), 519–27.

35 **Forbes magazine estimates:** Chase Peterson-Withorn, "Forbes' 36th Annual World's Billionaires List: Facts and Figures 2022," *Forbes,* April 5, 2022, www.forbes.com/sites/chasewithorn/2022/04/05/forbes-36th-annual-worlds-billionaires-list-facts-and-figures-2022.

35 **According to calculations by Forbes:** Rachel Sandler, "The Forbes Philanthropy Score 2022: How Charitable Are the Richest Americans?," *Forbes,* September 27, 2022, www.forbes.com/sites/rachelsandler/2022/09/27/the-forbes-philanthropy-score-2022-how-charitable-are-the-richest-americans/?sh=6d0efebfa098.

Chapter 4: Secret Superpowers

38 **When a video:** Sudeept Mishra, "Bhopal Braveheart Dives Under Moving Train to Save Girl, Heroism Caught on Camera," *Times of India,* February 11, 2022, https://timesofindia.indiatimes.com/city/bhopal/bhopal-braveheart-dives-under-moving-train-to-save-girl-heroism-caught-on-camera/articleshow/89515582.cms.

41 **For example, in one study:** Samuel L. Gaertner and John F. Dovidio, "The Common Ingroup Identity Model," in Paul A. M. Van Lange, Arie W. Kruglanski, and E. Tory Higgins, eds., *Handbook of Theories of Social Psychology,* vol. 2 (Thousand Oaks, CA: Sage Publications, 2012), 439–57.

41 **The widespread reading of novels:** Claudia Hammond, "Does Reading Fiction Make Us Better People?," BBC, June 3, 2019, www.bbc.com/future/article/20190523-does-reading-fiction-make-us-better-people.

44 **But in the case of generosity:** Jonathan Haidt, "Wired to Be Inspired," *Greater Good,* March 1, 2005, https://greatergood.berkeley
.edu/article/item/wired_to_be_inspired.

46 **Our instinctive self:** Daniel Kahneman, *Thinking, Fast and Slow* (London: Penguin, 2012), 20–30.

48 **The polling firm Gallup:** Data from Gallup World Poll 2013, www
.gallup.com/analytics/349487/gallup-global-happiness-center.aspx (closed access).

48 **In her TED Talk:** Elizabeth Dunn, "Helping others makes us happier—but it matters how we do it," TED, 2019, www.ted.com/
talks/elizabeth_dunn_helping_others_makes_us_happier_but_it
_matters_how_we_do_it.

49 **This creates a dangerous asymmetry:** Ed O'Brien and Samantha Kassirer, "People Are Slow to Adapt to the Warm Glow of Giving," *Psychological Science* 30, no. 2 (2019): 193–204.

Chapter 5: The Mystery Experiment

57 **It estimated that:** Ryan J. Dwyer and Elizabeth W. Dunn, "Wealth Distribution Promotes Happiness," *Proceedings of the National Academy of Sciences* 119, no. 46 (2022): 2–3.

Gratitude Break

62 **After a humiliating 360-degree review:** Dan Harris, "The benefits of not being a jerk to yourself," TED, 2022, www.ted.com/talks/dan
_harris_the_benefits_of_not_being_a_jerk_to_yourself.

64 **"Begin by opening your eyes":** Brother David Steindl-Rast, "Gratitude | Louie Schwartzberg | TEDxSF," YouTube, June 11, 2011, www.youtube.com/watch?v=gXDMoiEkyuQ.

Chapter 6: Six Ways to Give That Aren't About Money

68 **"In the hour that followed":** Joshua Coombes, *Do Something for Nothing: Seeing Beneath the Surface of Homelessness, Through the Simple Act of a Haircut* (London: Murdoch Books, 2021), 10.

69 **Joshua has garnered:** Instagram account @joshuacoombes has 156,000 followers as of June 2023.

69 **When Joshua posted:** Coombes, *Do Something for Nothing,* 106.

69 **"Give the benefit of the doubt":** Coombes, *Do Something for Nothing,* 219.

73 **"the way to skyrocket through the algorithm":** Dylan Marron, *Conver-*

sations with People Who Hate Me: 12 Things I Learned from Talking to Internet Strangers (New York: Atria Books, 2022), loc. 14, Kindle.

73 **"You're a piece of shit":** Marron, *Conversations with People Who Hate Me,* loc. 99.

73 **In his TED Talk:** Dylan Marron, "Empathy is not endorsement," TED, 2018, www.ted.com/talks/dylan_marron_empathy_is_not _endorsement.

74 **"the most subversive thing":** Marron, "Empathy is not endorsement."

74 **"Before I met Craig":** *Changed My Mind* podcast, "Becoming Friends with Your Arch Enemy with Leah Garcés," Spotify, June 2020, https:// open.spotify.com/episode/76PEwtrQrdD3MGzS0z15gV?si=826a6812 692247e2.

77 **Taiwan's inaugural minister:** Carl Miller, "Taiwan's Crowdsourced Democracy Shows Us How to Fix Social Media," Reasons to Be Cheerful, September 27, 2020, https://wearenotdivided.reasonstobecheerful .world/taiwan-g0v-hackers-technology-digital-democracy.

78 **Since then, their lessons:** Statistic from Khan Academy YouTube channel, www.youtube.com/@khanacademy.

80 **In her TED Talk:** Elizabeth Dunn, "Helping others makes us happier—but it matters how we do it," TED, 2019, www.ted.com/ talks/elizabeth_dunn_helping_others_makes_us_happier_but_it _matters_how_we_do_it.

82 **"I felt it":** Orahachi Onubedo, "Under the Hoodie—Ada Nduka Oyom, DevRel Ecosystem Community Manager with Google," BenjaminDada, July 20, 2021, www.benjamindada.com/under-the -hoodie-ada-nduka-oyom.

83 **As of 2023:** Statistic from She Code Africa website, https:// shecodeafrica.org/.

84 **He wrote that:** Rory Stewart, "Books: 'The Places in Between,'" *Washington Post,* August 10, 2006, www.washingtonpost.com/wp -dyn/content/discussion/2006/08/03/DI2006080300716.html.

84 **In his remarkable book:** Donald Brown, *Human Universals* (New York: McGraw-Hill, 1991), loc. 1500, Kindle.

85 **Even a decade ago:** Guy Trebay, "Guess Who Isn't Coming to Dinner," *New York Times,* November 28, 2012, www.nytimes.com/2012/ 11/29/fashion/saving-the-endangered-dinner-party.html.

87 **"I felt an emptiness inside":** TEDx Talks YouTube channel, "From broken to whole: Lily Yeh at TEDxCornellU," YouTube, December 20, 2013, www.youtube.com/watch?v=fVCXF6PN0g4.

88 **In 2020:** "An Artist Is Creating a Rainbow Square in Gloucester,"
BBC, May 13, 2022, www.bbc.co.uk/news/uk-england-gloucestershire
-61421731.

88 **In Lyon, France, an artist:** Ian Phillips, "France's Answer to Banksy:
The Anonymous Street Artist Filling Potholes with Colourful Mosaics,"
Guardian, September 11, 2022, www.theguardian.com/artanddesign/
2022/sep/11/frances-answer-to-banksy-the-anonymous-street-artist
-filling-potholes-with-colourful-mosaics-.

89 **Busy New Yorkers:** "The Sing for Hope Pianos on CBS Sunday
Morning," YouTube, SingForHope YouTube channel, February 3,
2022, www.youtube.com/watch?v=2kGLILDaeK0&t=1s.

89 **In locked-down Florence:** @MuhammadLila Twitter account, "During Italy's quarantine . . . ," March 14, 2020, https://twitter.com/
muhammadlila/status/1238671011698151427?s=21.

89 **In South Waziristan:** Asad Hashim, "Pakistan Musicians Fill Silence
in Former Taliban Stronghold," *Al Jazeera,* February 28, 2018, www
.aljazeera.com/features/2018/2/28/pakistan-musicians-fill-silence-in
-former-taliban-stronghold.

Chapter 7: Catalysts of Contagion

94 **For example, in 2022:** Elle Hunt, " 'They Filmed Me Without My
Consent': The Ugly Side of #Kindness Videos," *Guardian,* January
31, 2023, www.theguardian.com/technology/2023/jan/31/they
-filmed-me-without-my-consent-the-ugly-side-of-kindness-videos.

94 **All the money he gets:** @MrBeast Twitter account, "Twitter—Rich
people should help others . . . ," Twitter, January 30, 2023, https://
twitter.com/MrBeast/status/1620195967008907264.

96 **A group of friends:** Heather Wake, "The Way These 'Samurai Litter
Pickers' Clean the Streets Is Kinda the Coolest Thing Ever," Upworthy, July 2, 2022, www.upworthy.com/samurai-litter-pickers-japan.

96 **As Mundano spray-painted:** Mundano, "Trash cart superheroes,"
TED, 2014, www.ted.com/talks/mundano_trash_cart_superheroes.

97 **Mockus could have responded:** Mara Cristina Caballero, "Academic
Turns City into a Social Experiment," *Harvard Gazette,* March 11,
2004, https://news.harvard.edu/gazette/story/2004/03/academic
-turns-city-into-a-social-experiment.

98 **During Mockus's leadership:** Caballero, "Academic Turns City into
a Social Experiment."

98 **Some critics think:** "Ice Bucket Challenge Dramatically Accelerated

the Fight Against ALS," ALS Association, June 4, 2019, www.als.org/
stories-news/ice-bucket-challenge-dramatically-accelerated-fight
-against-als.

99　**The humor and the personal engagement:** "About Us—Financials,"
Movember, 2022, https://us.movember.com/about/money.

100　**CNN heard about this strange relationship:** Mallory Simon and Sara
Sidner, "What Happened When a Klansman Met a Black Man in
Charlottesville," CNN, July 16, 2020, https://edition.cnn.com/2017/
12/15/us/charlottesville-klansman-black-man-meeting/index.html.

100　**As he said:** TEDx Talks YouTube channel, "Why I, as a black man,
attend KKK rallies | Daryl Davis | TEDxNaperville," YouTube, De-
cember 8, 2017, www.youtube.com/watch?v=ORp3q1Oaezw.

100　**It sometimes burns bright:** "Mamoudou Gassama: Mali 'Spiderman'
Becomes French Citizen," BBC, September 13, 2018, www.bbc.co
.uk/news/world-europe-45507663.

100　**And it sometimes has:** Sirin Kale, "'He's a Hero'—the Teacher Who
Hand-Delivered 15,000 Free School Meals in Lockdown," *Guardian,*
November 13, 2021, www.theguardian.com/lifeandstyle/2021/nov/13/
hes-a-hero-the-teacher-who-hand-delivered-15000-free-school-meals-in
-lockdown.

100　**When Covid hit the UK:** "Obituary: Captain Sir Tom Moore, a Hero
Who Gave a Nation Hope," BBC, February 2, 2021, www.bbc.co.uk/
news/uk-52726188.

102　**The Grammy-winning:** Claire Schafer, "OK Go Premiere New Song
for Frontline COVID-19 Workers," *Rolling Stone,* May 13, 2020, www
.rollingstone.com/music/music-news/ok-go-all-together-now-covid
-19-998665/.

103　**Deeply moved:** OK Go YouTube account, "OK Go Sandbox—Behind
the Scenes of #ArtTogetherNow," YouTube, 2021, www.youtube.com/
watch?v=W0S7SA6DVfk&t=335s.

104　**By 2020:** Mark Savage, "BTS Were the Top-Selling Act in the World
Last Year," BBC, February 24, 2022, www.bbc.co.uk/news/entertainment
-arts-60505910.

104　**To celebrate the birthdays:** @KimNamjoonPHL Twitter account,
"Plant Today, Save Tomorrow . . . ," Twitter, September 8, 2019,
https://twitter.com/KimNamjoonPHL/status/1170581124646457344
?s=20.

104　**Thousands of native trees:** "BTS Fans Build Forest in RM's Name as
Birthday Gift," *Soompi,* September 3, 2019, www.soompi.com/

article/1349882wpp/bts-fans-build-forest-in-rms-name-as-birthday
-gift; AllKPop user btsarmykook, " 'BTS Jungkook Forest No. 4' Created by Fans to Improve Biodiversity in Collaboration with the Korean Federation for Environmental Movement," AllKPop, November 19,
2021, www.allkpop.com/article/2021/11/bts-jungkook-forest-no-4
-created-by-fans-to-improve-biodiversity-in-collaboration-with-the
-korean-federation-for-environmental-movement.

105 **The International Network of Crisis Mappers:** Statistics from International Network of Crisis Mappers website, http://crisismapping
.ning.com.

109 **In the spring of 2017:** *Sounds Good* podcast, "3 Myths About Changing
the World," April 5, 2021, www.goodgoodgood.co/podcast/amy-wolff-3
-myths-about-changing-the-world.

110 **Wolff didn't make a cent:** *Sounds Good* podcast, "3 Myths About
Changing the World."

Chapter 8: Pass It On!

112 **"Human progress is not":** Email correspondence between author
and Steven Pinker, March 3, 2023.

113 **When you take all causes:** Max Roser, Hannah Ritchie, Esteban
Ortiz-Ospina, and Lucas Rodés-Guirao, "World Population
Growth," Our World in Data, 2023, https://ourworldindata.org/
world-population-growth.

113 **To take just one example:** Global Health Observatory, "Child Mortality and Causes of Death," World Health Organization, 2023, www
.who.int/data/gho/data/themes/topics/topic-details/GHO/child
-mortality-and-causes-of-death.

114 **A classic social psychology paper:** Roy F. Baumeister and Ellen
Bratslavsky, "Bad Is Stronger Than Good," *Review of General Psychology* 5, no. 4 (2001): 323–70.

116 **Yet penicillin would play:** Peter Hogg, "Top 10 Most Important
Drugs in History," *Proclinical*, January 18, 2022, www.proclinical
.com/blogs/2022-1/top-10-most-important-drugs-in-history.

121 **She quickly committed:** Nick Statt, "MacKenzie Scott Has Already
Donated Nearly $1.7 Billion of Her Amazon Wealth Since Divorcing
Jeff Bezos," *The Verge*, July 28, 2020, www.theverge.com/2020/7/28/
21345440/mackenzie-scott-jeff-bezos-amazon-wealth-donation
-philanthropy.

121 **"It was the local dentist":** MacKenzie Scott, "No Dollar Signs This Time," Yield Giving, December 8, 2021, https://yieldgiving.com/essays/no-dollar-signs-this-time.

Chapter 9: And What About Money?

124 **In Tibetan Buddhism:** Derek Beres, "Idiot Compassion and Mindfulness," Big Think, October 30, 2013, https://bigthink.com/articles/idiot-compassion-and-mindfulness/.

129 **In the United States and Europe:** Austin Frakt, "Putting a Dollar Value on Life? Governments Already Do," *New York Times,* May 11, 2020, www.nytimes.com/2020/05/11/upshot/virus-price-human-life.html.

129 **But, according to givewell.org:** "How We Produce Impact Estimates," GiveWell, April 2023, www.givewell.org/impact-estimates.

133 **For about $70:** Statistic from KickStart website, https://kickstart.org/how-we-work/; "KickStart MoneyMaker Hip Pump," Engineering for Change, 2023, www.engineeringforchange.org/solutions/product/moneymaker-hip-pump/.

133 **Even after taking into account:** *2022 Annual Report,* KickStart, June 2023, 3, https://kickstart.org/wp-content/uploads/2023/06/2022_KickStart-Annual-Report-1.pdf.

133 **Ninety million dollars. That's leverage:** David W. Brown, "A Security Camera for the Planet," *New Yorker,* April 28, 2023, www.newyorker.com/news/annals-of-climate-action/a-security-camera-for-the-planet.

134 **In philanthropic terms:** Safeena Husain, "A bold plan to empower 1.6 million out-of-school girls in India," TED, 2019, www.ted.com/talks/safeena_husain_a_bold_plan_to_empower_1_6_million_out_of_school_girls_in_india.

135 **After countless setbacks:** "Lighting the Way: Roadmaps to Exits in Off-Grid Energy," Acumen, 2019, 18, https://acumen.org/wp-content/uploads/acumen-exits-off-grid-energy-report.pdf.

136 **Eighty public-benefit programs:** Amanda Renteria, "A bold plan to transform access to the US social safety net," TED, 2022, www.ted.com/talks/amanda_renteria_a_bold_plan_to_transform_access_to_the_us_social_safety_net.

136 **To take a typical example:** Renteria, "A bold plan to transform access to the US social safety net."

136 **When the pandemic hit:** Renteria, "A bold plan to transform access to the US social safety net."

137 **With the support of national health systems:** Raj Panjabi, "No one should die because they live too far from a doctor," TED, 2017, www.ted.com/talks/raj_panjabi_no_one_should_die_because_they_live_too_far_from_a_doctor/transcript.

139 **Patreon allows millions:** "The Story of Patreon," Patreon, 2023, www.patreon.com/about.

140 **Today hundreds of thousands:** *Unleashing Generosity Globally: 2022 Impact Report,* GivingTuesday, 2023, 22, https://issuu.com/givingtues/docs/2022_givingtuesdayimpactreportfinal.

140 **The donors who fund:** Based on email correspondence with Giving-Tuesday.

Chapter 10: The Internet We Want

146 **"We're facing 25 years":** Peter Schwartz and Peter Leyden, "The Long Boom: A History of the Future, 1980–2020," *Wired,* July 1, 1997, www.wired.com/1997/07/longboom.

146 **In 2010, I gave a TED Talk:** Chris Anderson, "How web video powers global innovation," TED, 2010, www.ted.com/talks/chris_anderson_how_web_video_powers_global_innovation.

147 **When he failed to get:** Roger McNamee, "How Facebook and Google Threaten Public Health—and Democracy," *Guardian,* November 11, 2017, www.theguardian.com/commentisfree/2017/nov/11/facebook-google-public-health-democracy.

147 **A year later, Nick Bostrom:** Nick Bostrom, "What happens when our computers get smarter than we are?," TED, 2015, www.ted.com/talks/nick_bostrom_what_happens_when_our_computers_get_smarter_than_we_are.

148 **At TED in 2017:** Tristan Harris, "How a handful of tech companies control billions of minds every day," TED, 2017, www.ted.com/talks/tristan_harris_how_a_handful_of_tech_companies_control_billions_of_minds_every_day.

148 **The following year at TED:** Jaron Lanier, "How we need to remake the internet," TED, 2018, www.ted.com/talks/jaron_lanier_how_we_need_to_remake_the_internet.

148 **And in 2019:** Carole Cadwalladr, "Facebook's role in Brexit—and the threat to democracy," TED, 2019, www.ted.com/talks/carole

_cadwalladr_facebook_s_role_in_brexit_and_the_threat_to
_democracy.

148 **Every day we query:** Maryam Mohsin, "10 Google Search Statistics You Need to Know," *Oberlo* (blog), January 13, 2023, www.oberlo.com/ blog/google-search-statistics; Peter Dizikes, "Why Social Media Has Changed the World—and How to Fix It," *MIT News*, September 24, 2020, https://news.mit.edu/2020/hype-machine-book-aral-0924; Manish Singh, "WhatsApp Is Now Delivering Roughly 100 Billion Messages a Day," *TechCrunch*, October 30, 2020, https://techcrunch.com/2020/ 10/29/whatsapp-is-now-delivering-roughly-100-billion-messages-a-day/.

150 **A shocking report in the UK:** "How Long Do Brits Spend Scrolling Through Their Phones?," Lenstore, January 11, 2022, www.lenstore .co.uk/eyecare/how-long-do-brits-spend-on-their-phones.

153 **According to researchers:** Matthew Williams, *The Science of Hate: How Prejudice Becomes Hate and What We Can Do to Stop It* (London: Faber and Faber, 2021), loc. 351, Kindle.

154 **Following the Brexit vote:** Williams, *The Science of Hate*, loc. 350.

154 **Here are some:** Williams, *The Science of Hate*, loc. 351.

156 **After one such announcement:** Michelle Castillo, "Facebook Plunges More Than 24 Percent on Revenue Miss and Projected Slowdown," CNBC, July 25, 2018, www.cnbc.com/2018/07/25/ facebook-earnings-q2-2018.html.

157 **A hopeful moment:** Twitter user @elonmusk, "New Twitter will strive . . . ," Twitter, December 30, 2022, https://twitter.com/ elonmusk/status/1608663342956302337.

159 **In China:** "China: Children Given Daily Time Limit on Douyin—Its Version of TikTok," BBC, September 20, 2021, www.bbc.co.uk/ news/technology-58625934.

162 **One of the most persuasive arguments:** Stuart Russell, "3 principles for creating safer AI," TED, 2017, www.ted.com/talks/stuart_russell _3_principles_for_creating_safer_ai.

Chapter 11: The Brilliant Move Companies Could Make

168 **But in 2018:** Jim Hagemann Snabe, "Dreams and details for a decarbonized future," TED, 2022, www.ted.com/talks/jim_hagemann _snabe_dreams_and_details_for_a_decarbonized_future.

168 **Since no one had an answer:** Snabe, "Dreams and details for a decarbonized future."

170 **In 2016, he had two thousand people:** Sam Thielman, "Chobani Millionaires: Employees Could Split 10% of Yogurt Company Windfall," *Guardian,* April 26, 2016, www.theguardian.com/business/2016/apr/26/chobani-employee-shares-yogurt-public.

170 **It has become:** Matthew Johnstone, "Chobani IPO: What You Need to Know," Investopedia, November 18, 2021, www.investopedia.com/chobani-ipo-what-you-need-to-know-5210079.

170 **In his TED Talk:** Hamdi Ulukaya, "The anti-CEO playbook," TED, 2019, www.ted.com/talks/hamdi_ulukaya_the_anti_ceo_playbook.

171 **A survey in late 2022:** Martin Armstrong, "The Size of the Company 'Given Away' to Save the Planet," Statista, September 15, 2022, www.statista.com/chart/28257/patagonia-inc-revenue-company-db/; "The Top 15 Coolest Clothing Brands According to Gen Z and Millennials," YPulse, August 18, 2022, www.ypulse.com/article/2022/08/18/the-top-15-coolest-clothing-brands-according-to-gen-z-and-millennials/.

Chapter 12: Philanthropy's True Potential

177 **For example, in technology:** Data from companiesmarketcap.com, https://companiesmarketcap.com/tech/largest-tech-companies-by-market-cap/.

182 **And in early 2023:** "More Than $1B Catalyzed for 2023 Audacious Projects," *TEDBlog,* April 27, 2023, https://blog.ted.com/2023-audacious-projects/.

Chapter 13: The Pledge That Could Change Everything

193 **Numerous charities out there:** "Our Top Charities," GiveWell, December 2022, www.givewell.org/charities/top-charities.

Chapter 14: Over to You

213 **Here are just a few:** All posts from the Kindness Pandemic Facebook page, www.facebook.com/groups/515507852491119.

ABOUT THE AUTHOR

CHRIS ANDERSON is an entrepreneur who has been leading the TED organization since 2001, overseeing the global spread of TED Talks. He also initiated The Audacious Project, which has raised several billion dollars for bold nonprofit initiatives. He lives in New York City and London.

infectiousgenerosity.org

Social media: @TEDchris